An opinionated guide to

PARIS

Written by

JOEL HART

Candle Kids Coffee (no.24)

INFORMATION IS DEAD. LONG LIVE OPINION.

Who needs a guidebook when everything can be googled for free and ChatGPT can tell you what you want? Because in an increasingly virtual world, you want lively, trustworthy *human* opinion. You don't want endless information from a thousand bots.

We think you are like us: you care about quality, you care about taste, you care about provenance, but you don't have time to waste on long words like 'provenance'. You want to cut to the chase: where's good?

We are an independent from east London. How dare we write a book about Paris? Because we work with passionate local writers who seek out the spots that remind us of the east London we know and love: these are the most creative, diverse and exciting places of all.

Parc Rives de Seine (no.70)

Nonette Bánh Mì & Donuts (no.27)
Opposite: Marin Montagut (no.32)

Haussmann apartments

Opposite: Tour d'Eiffel (not in this book, but you won't miss it)

PARIS IS ALWAYS A GOOD IDEA

Is it a cliché to call Paris the most romantic city in the world? Absolutely. But isn't it also true? Long considered the *cité de l'amour*, so many lovers attached padlocks to the Pont des Arts over the years that the weight threatened to pull the entire bridge down. But Paris is more than a honeymoon destination, and the romance it evokes goes beyond that of love affairs. It has always been fertile ground for writers, artists, philosophers, revolutionaries and dreamers, from the elegance of the Belle Époque to the angst of the Lost Generation.

Think of Paris and you are probably picturing row upon row of pretty, pastel-hued Haussmann apartments, traditional bistros, the Eiffel Tower at sunset... but the real city is both magical and gritty, its charm lying precisely in this tension. Whether it's the weathered bohemianism of Belleville or the layered panoramic views in Parc des Buttes-Chaumont (no.69), you don't have to go far to find this electrifying juxtaposition.

Paris has never been so diverse as it is today. The city's global demographic – nearly half of the population are first- or second-generation immigrants – is reflected in the dynamic cultural programming of its art institutions, from the Brutalist Bourse de Commerce (no.52), championing diasporic artists, to the Philharmonie de Paris (no.62), showcasing everything from Beethoven symphonies to Malian Kora music.

And there's nowhere where this diversity is better emphasised than in how the city eats. Long the lodestar of gourmands, the last 30 years have seen Parisian dining culture shift from gastronomically conservative to groundbreaking. Bistros like Le Servan (no.16) fuse French ingredients with Asian influences, while Cheval d'Or (no.5) rethinks classic French cooking through a Chinese lens.

There may be no greater place on earth to surrender to over-indulgence, but for those inclined to resist A. J. Liebling-style gluttony, there are endless other ways to explore the city. From the independent boutiques of the Marais to the overgrown abandoned railway line – now a walkway – that circles the city (no.68), it pays to meander on foot. It's no coincidence that the term *flâneur* – meaning the aimless urban wanderer – originates here (with the poet and critic Baudelaire).

Let yourself be beguiled by the city's uniquely independent spirit: historic shopfronts and Gothic spires, Art Nouveau balconies and Brutalist housing blocks. There's bad taste everywhere on this planet, but a lot less of it in Paris. Whether you're a lucky resident or a regular visitor like me, the city stays with you. As Hemingway put it, 'Paris is a moveable feast'.

Joel Hart
Paris, 2025

Joel Hart is a writer, urban anthropologist and culture journalist with a focus on restaurants, wine and gastronomic travel. His work has appeared in the Financial Times, The Observer and more. You can find him on Instagram @joelhart.

BEST FOR...

Timeless Paris

Amble through the covered Passage des Panoramas (no.58), an 18th-century arcade of artisan shops, or wind upwards through Montmartre to the Sacré-Cœur (no.60) for breathtaking views across the city's rooftops. For dinner, Chez Georges (no.11) and Robert et Louise (no.12) radiate old-world charm.

Art

The Louvre (no.51) is unsurpassable, but if a visit feels overwhelming, head to the Musée Rodin (no.66) to zone in on the father of modern sculpture, or the Musée d'Orsay (no.50) for a mind-blowing display of Impressionist heavyweights.

Indie shopping

Try Papier Tigre (no.42) for chic stationery and Shakespeare and Company (no.36) for English books. If you're looking to bring some gourmet goodies home, head to Lemon Story (no.39) for marmalade-style jams and citrus-infused biscuits.

Cutting-edge fine dining

The French invented haute cuisine – and to this day, no one does it better. Septime (no.13) stretches the boundaries of modern French food, plating up thoughtful, plant-focused dishes, while AT (no.18) blends French, Japanese, Nordic and Spanish influences. For something more opulent, head to Le Clarence (no.4), where the grand dining room contrasts with a progressive, seafood-focused menu and cutting-edge wine list.

Pastries

What are you doing in Paris if not stuffing your face with pâtisserie? The choux à la flouve (cream-filled bun) from Tapisserie (no.10) is one of the city's essential bites. For purists, Maison d'Isabelle (no.22) offers award-winning butter croissants.

With kids

The best parks for letting loose your little ones are Parc des Buttes-Chaumont (no.69), which hosts puppet shows at Théâtre Guignol Anatole, and Parc Monceau (no.73), with several activity zones. And nothing beats a pit stop at ice cream bar Folderol (no.9), where you can get a glass of wine, too.

Visiting on a budget

In the city that gave rise to the prix fixe, Café du Coin (no.1) offers one of the best-value versions, while Caractère du Cochon (no.28) is a top spot for a hearty jambon-beurre (ham and butter baguette). Grab one to fuel you for a stroll along the vibrant urban waterway, Canal Saint-Martin (no.72).

Natural wine

Le Baratin (no.30) and Bistrot des Tournelles (no.2) feature sought-after natural wine producers, while the inimitable Bistrot Paul Bert (no.19) has a cellar stacked with older vintages. Before you leave the city, drop by La Cave Pigalle (no.40) to pick up a magnificent bottle to bring home.

A PERFECT WEEKEND

Friday night

Any weekend in Paris should begin with a dose of Gallic delights. If you're arriving by Eurostar, head to nearby Les Arlots (no.3) to tuck into their famous saucisse-purée (sausage and mash), or to the impossibly charming Chez Georges (no.11) for escargot (snails) and entrecôte (ribeye steak). Both restaurants should be reserved by phone.

Saturday morning

Shake off last night's indulgence with a ramble through Père Lachaise (no.67), paying your respects at the graves of Oscar Wilde and Jim Morrison. Then make your way to Rond (no.29) for superlative galettes and crêpes and an excellent view of the city from the top of nearby Parc de Belleville.

Saturday afternoon

A pastry overdose is obligatory on any Paris trip, so hop on the Metro to Mamiche (no.8) for next-level babka and other delights. Walk it off with a stroll up to Montmartre to pick up some citrusy treats at Lemon Story (no.39), before making your way to the unforgettable Sacré-Cœur (no.60).

Saturday evening

Aim for a reservation at Le Servan (no.16) or Maison Sota (no.6) for jaw-droppingly creative cuisine, before heading over to Fréquence (no.85) to get merry on highballs and dance until the early hours.

Sunday morning

After a leisurely coffee at Tanat (no.25) and a visit to Sainte-Chapelle (no.65) nearby, continue to seize the day with a bit of museum-hopping. You can enter the heavy-hitting Musée de l'Orangerie (no.54) and Musée d'Orsay (no.50) on a double ticket and they're both free to visit on the first Sunday of every month.

Sunday midday

Walk along the Parc Rives de Seine (no.70) to work up an appetite for lunch at Marché des Enfants Rouges (no.14), the city's oldest food market, boasting a mouthwatering array of options.

Sunday afternoon

Wander through the Jewish quarter – perhaps stopping by the Picasso Museum (no.53) if you still have one in you – before ambling to the Upper Marais to browse stylish, design-led gifts at Papier Tigre (no.42) and Yvon Lambert (no.41).

Sunday evening

For a casual early-evening bite, the nearby Delicatessen Cave (no.17) serves small plates from some of the city's buzziest resident chefs until 8pm. But for a truly unforgettable ending, make your way to AT (no.18) for a masterful tasting menu.

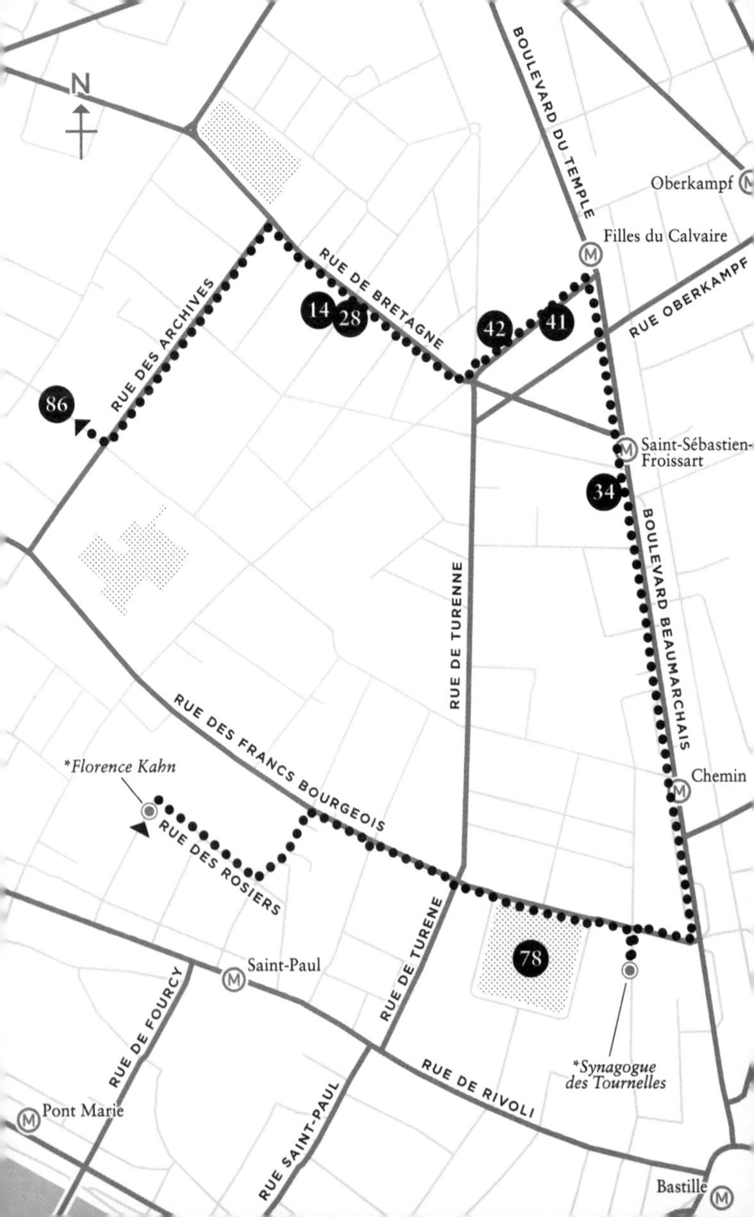
N
BOULEVARD DU TEMPLE
Oberkampf
Filles du Calvaire
RUE OBERKAMPF
RUE DE BRETAGNE
RUE DES ARCHIVES
14
28
42
41
86
Saint-Sébastien-Froissart
34
BOULEVARD BEAUMARCHAIS
RUE DE TURENNE
RUE DES FRANCS BOURGEOIS
*Florence Kahn
RUE DES ROSIERS
Chemin
78
Saint-Paul
RUE DE TURENE
RUE DE FOURCY
*Synagogue des Tournelles
RUE DE RIVOLI
Pont Marie
RUE SAINT-PAUL
Bastille

WALK 1: LE MARAIS

Stroll through the historic Jewish quarter

Start on rue des Rosiers, the heart of the city's most famous Jewish neighbourhood, known as the Pletzl (Yiddish for 'little place'). The street is home to several historic businesses, such as Florence Kahn* – a mosaic-fronted Jewish bakery and deli serving delectable poppy-seed cheesecake and strudel. Walk east via Place des Vosges 78 – the oldest planned square in Paris – to the Synagogue des Tournelles*, a cornerstone of the Pletzl. Head north on boulevard Beaumarchais towards the indie shopping hub of Upper Marais, visiting Merci 34, Yvon Lambert 41 and Papier Tigre 42 for quirky gifts. Laden with souvenirs, walk west along rue de Bretagne towards lunch: either Caractère de Cochon 28 for a jambon-stuffed baguette, or Marché des Enfants Rouges 14 for some majestic seafood dishes at Les Enfants du Marché, or a box of pretty much any street food your heart desires from one of the many stalls. Finish up at Bar Nouveau 86 for a well-earned afternoon cocktail.

Walking time: 40 mins, 2.6 km

Total time with stops: 2–3 hours

*(*Location not in guidebook: more info online)*

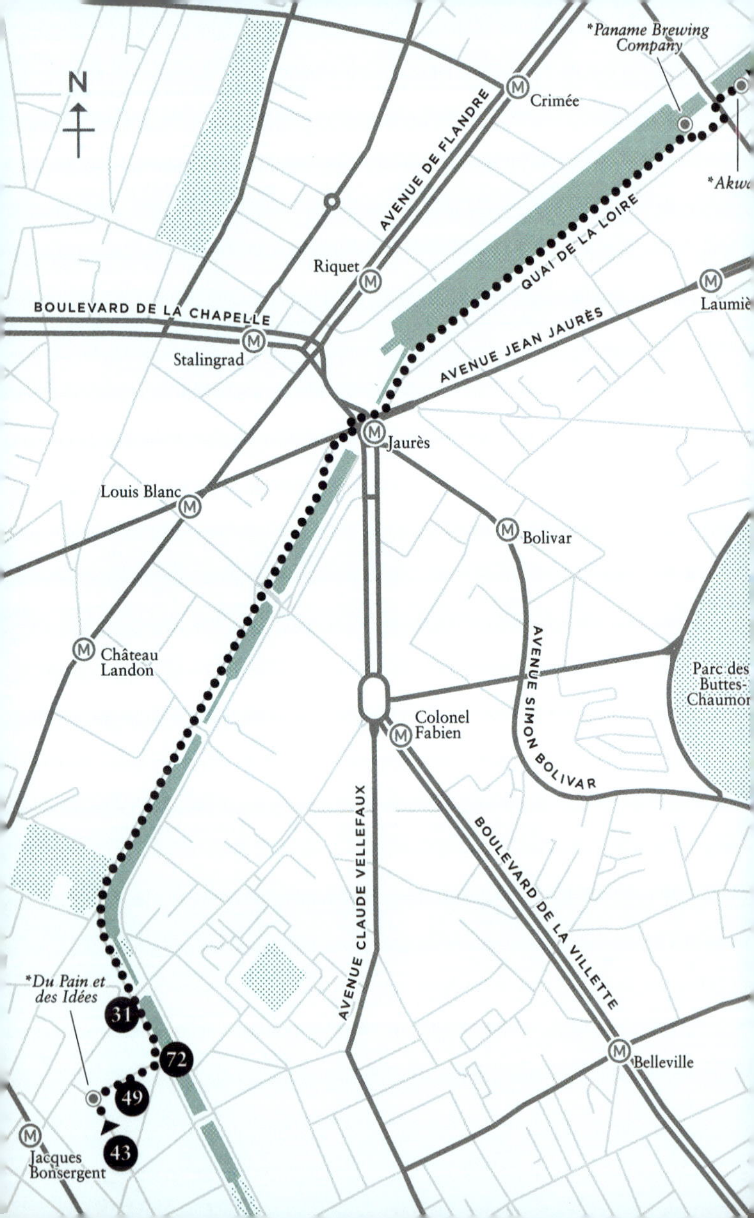
N
*Paname Brewing Company
Crimée
*Akw
AVENUE DE FLANDRE
QUAI DE LA LOIRE
Riquet
Laumiè
BOULEVARD DE LA CHAPELLE
Stalingrad
AVENUE JEAN JAURÈS
Jaurès
Louis Blanc
Bolivar
Château Landon
AVENUE SIMON BOLIVAR
Parc des Buttes-Chaumon
Colonel Fabien
AVENUE CLAUDE VELLEFAUX
BOULEVARD DE LA VILLETTE
*Du Pain et des Idées
31
72
49
43
Belleville
Jacques Bonsergent

WALK 2: CANAL SAINT-MARTIN

Indie shopping and grazing from canal to canal

Caffeinate yourself at the achingly cool design shop Bonjour Jacob 43, where you can also leaf through some magazines, before continuing up the road to Du Pain et des Idées*, a traditional boulangerie serving exceptionally good pistachio swirls. Sated? Just around the corner is Centre Commercial 49, offering a curated selection of sustainable clothes and homeware. Walk down rue de Marseille until you hit the Canal Saint-Martin 72, then left up quai de Valmy to visit Artazart 31, home to a brilliant selection of affordably priced wall prints. Once you're done shopping, continue along the water's edge for about half an hour, enjoying the relaxed energy and sounds of buskers playing on the banks. Once you get to rue La Fayette, cross over the main road and back onto the canal path on the other side. The canal opens out at the Bassin de la Villette. Stop here for a pint at Paname Brewing Company*, before continuing onto Canal de l'Ourcq, where you can rent an electric boat with Akwa* – the ideal scenario for a sunny day picnic and a bottle of Provençal rosé.

Walking time: 40 mins, 2.6 km

Total time with stops: 2–4 hours

*(*Location not in guidebook: more info online)*

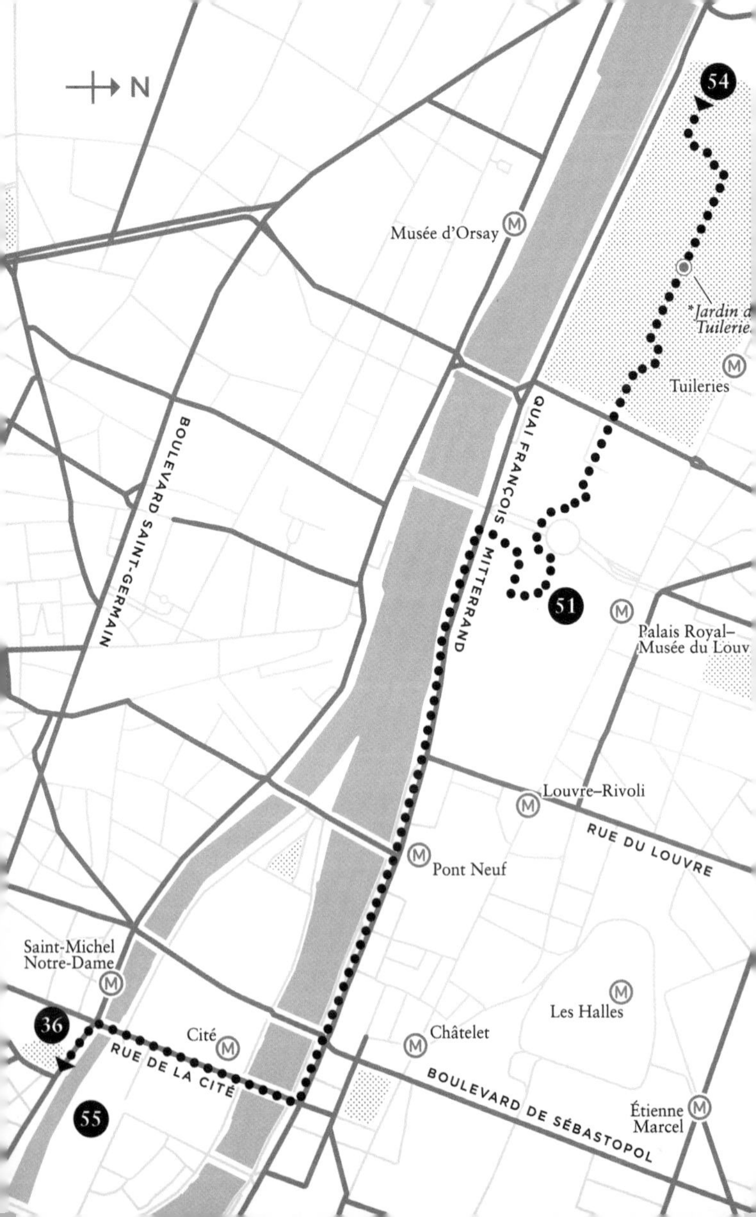
N
54
Musée d'Orsay
*Jardin d
Tuilerie
Tuileries
BOULEVARD SAINT-GERMAIN
QUAI FRANÇOIS MITTERRAND
51
Palais Royal–
Musée du Louv
Louvre–Rivoli
RUE DU LOUVRE
Pont Neuf
Saint-Michel
Notre-Dame
Les Halles
36
Cité
Châtelet
RUE DE LA CITÉ
BOULEVARD DE SÉBASTOPOL
Étienne
Marcel
55

WALK 3: ALONG THE SEINE

Tour of the city's cultural treasures

After a visit to Monet's mesmerising *Water Lilies* at Musée de l'Orangerie 54, make your way through the manicured lanes of the Jardin des Tuileries*. Glide past I.M. Pei's iconic glass pyramid marking the entrance to the Louvre 51 on your way to the quai du Louvre. From here, follow the river eastward, tracing the Seine along the shaded banks past the iconic *bouquinistes* – forest-green stalls selling old books, art prints and faux-vintage posters. Keep straight on until you reach Pont Notre-Dame and a view of the cathedral's stunning towers rising just across the river. Cross the water here, past Notre-Dame 55 itself and onto the Left Bank and the Latin Quarter. Historically associated with the city's bohemian artist population, the Latin Quarter today is a convivial district of cobbled streets, Sorbonne university buildings and bookshops. Shakespeare and Company 36 is the most famous, with the queue often visible from across the Seine. Browse its warren of shelving packed with second-hand gems before refuelling in the shop's cafe next door.

Walking time: 45 mins, 3 km

Total time with stops: 2–3 hours

*(*Location not in guidebook: more info online)*

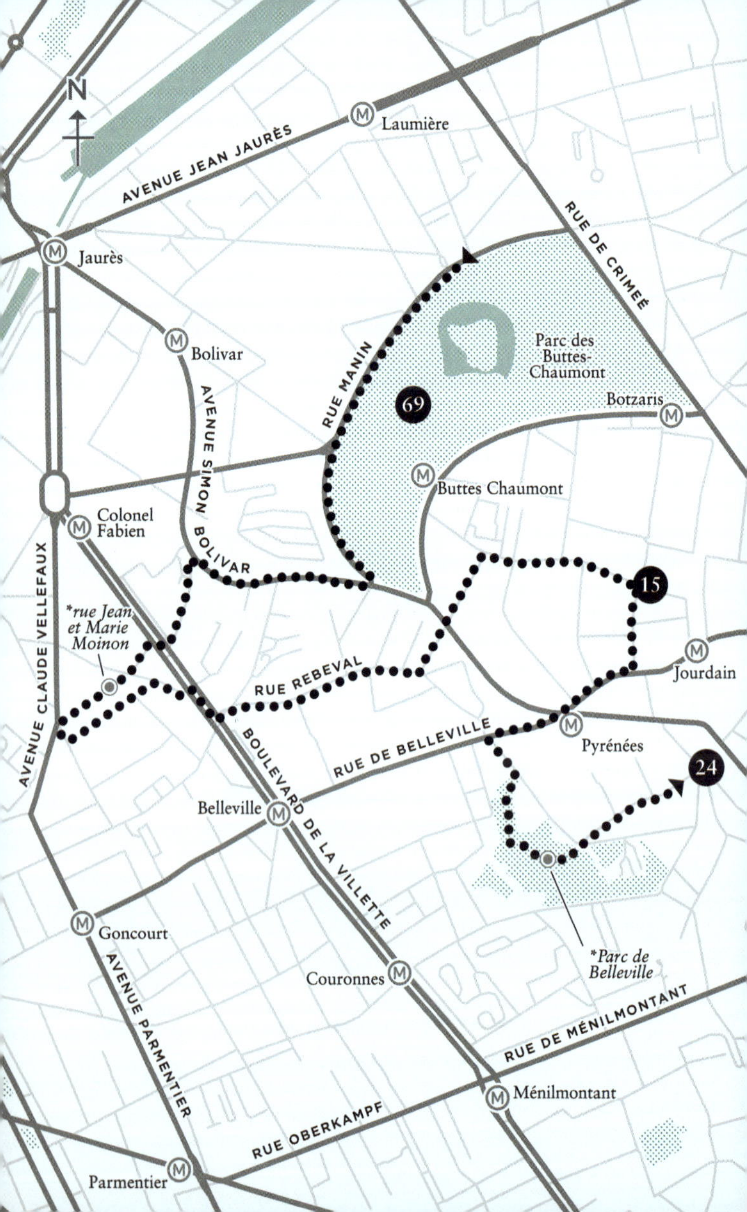
N
Laumière
AVENUE JEAN JAURÈS
Jaurès
RUE DE CRIMEÉ
Parc des
Buttes-
Chaumont
Bolivar
RUE MANIN
69
Botzaris
AVENUE SIMON BOLIVAR
Buttes Chaumont
Colonel
Fabien
15
*rue Jean
et Marie
Moinon
RUE REBEVAL
Jourdain
AVENUE CLAUDE VELLEFAUX
RUE DE BELLEVILLE
Pyrénées
24
BOULEVARD DE LA VILLETTE
Belleville
Goncourt
Couronnes
*Parc de
Belleville
AVENUE PARMENTIER
RUE DE MÉNILMONTANT
Ménilmontant
RUE OBERKAMPF
Parmentier

WALK 4: BELLEVILLE

Live like a local

Begin your morning saunter around the enchanting Parc des Buttes-Chaumont 69, home to a waterfall, a lake and the moss-covered monument, the Temple de la Sybille. Then weave your way west towards rue Jean et Marie Moinon* – known as the ateliers' street – where creativity spills out from every doorway. This area is a hotspot for artists' studios, and the Ateliers d'Artistes de Belleville (AAB) host regular events and annual open days (usually in May) when the doors to their workshops are flung open to the public. Walk south from here and back east along rue Rébeval towards the leafy enclave of Village Jourdain – home to buzzy street markets, petite art galleries and residential buildings – for a seafood-forward lunch at Soces 15. Once you've gorged on oyster platters and tuna crudo to your heart's content, walk it off with a loop around Parc de Belleville*, enjoying its stirring panoramic city views. Finish up with a coffee and a canelé at Candle Kids 24 – a peaceful spot where you can park up for an hour with a good book.

Walking time: 1 hour, 5 km

Total time with stops: 3.5–4.5 hours

*(*Location not in guidebook: more info online)*

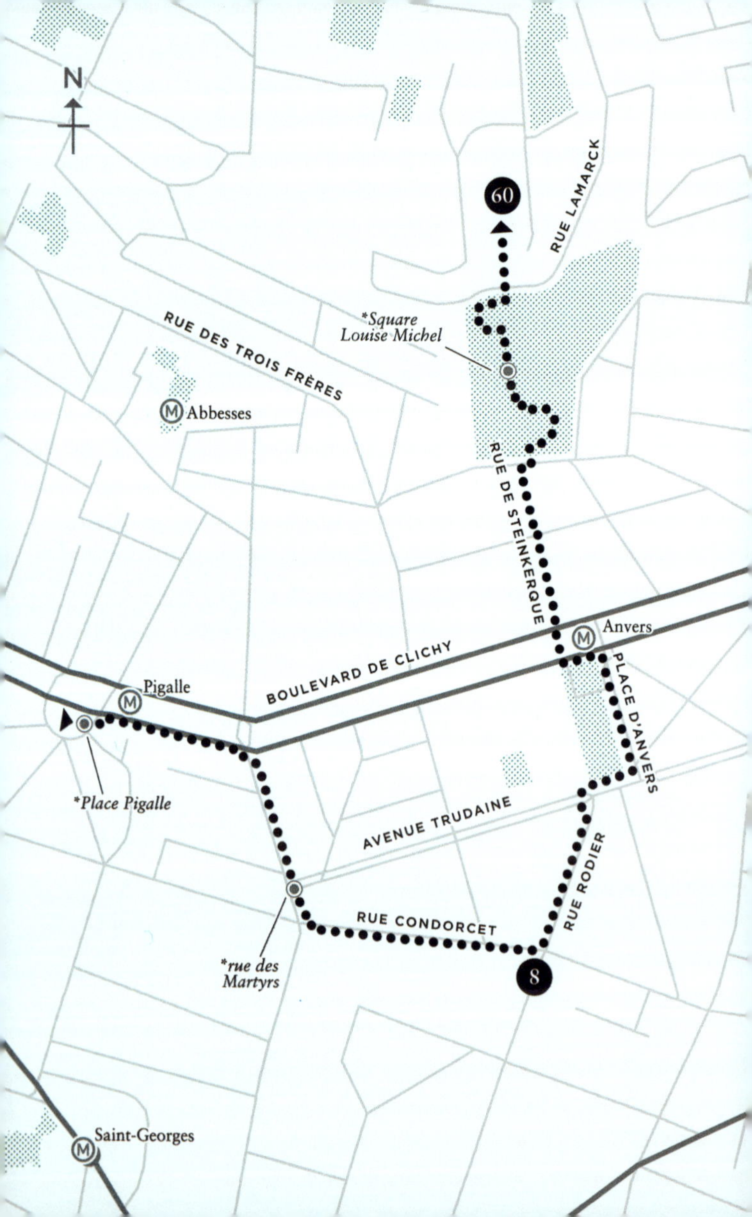
N
60
RUE LAMARCK
*Square
Louise Michel
RUE DES TROIS FRÈRES
Abbesses
RUE DE STEINKERQUE
Anvers
BOULEVARD DE CLICHY
Pigalle
PLACE D'ANVERS
*Place Pigalle
AVENUE TRUDAINE
RUE RODIER
RUE CONDORCET
*rue des
Martyrs
8
Saint-Georges

WALK 5: MONTMARTRE

From Pigalle to the peak of Paris

Start at Place Pigalle*, once the heart of the city's seedy underbelly of cabarets, clubs and sex shops, and now a creative, cafe-dense area popular with a young crowd. Walk east, down rue des Martyrs* – a lively, sloping street lined with florists, wine caves and charming *épiceries* (groceries) – towards Mamiche ❽, where you can secure a doorstep sandwich and a couple of sweet treats. Head north towards Square Louise Michel*, the terraced park that unfolds beneath Sacré-Cœur (60). Pause here for a breather and to scoff those Mamiche goodies. If you've got kids in tow, consider taking the Montmartre funicular up to the Sacré-Cœur itself – or you can brave the 222 exhausting steps and be rewarded by the city's best view.

Walking time: 30 mins, 1.5 km

Total time with stops: 1.5–2 hours

*(*Location not in guidebook: more info online)*

1

CAFÉ DU COIN

Progressive prix fixe

There's no gloopy French onion soup or steak frites in sight at this offbeat restaurant. The intriguing cuisine feels distinctly French but undeniably lighter than classic bistro fare – and at €18–21, the *prix fixe* lunch menu is a steal. Enjoy cuttlefish croque with eel cream and sorrel, or caramelised scallops with hollandaise and feijoa fruit. Water is poured from repurposed Ricard bottles, and you can sit on the terrace in warmer months. Reservations are only available at lunch, but it's worth swinging by in the evening, when there are small plates and pizzettes laden with smoked mozzarella and za'atar, or lardo, taleggio and egg.

9 rue Camille Desmoulins, 75011
Nearest Metro: Voltaire
instagram.com/cafe_du_coin

35

2

BISTROT DES TOURNELLES

Classic bistro with exquisite interiors

If you're not beguiled by the impeccable facade of this restaurant, then you're probably in the wrong city. Many people will tell you to go to Bistrot des Tournelles for the top-notch grub – they're not wrong (the bistro food is classic and comforting), but it's the restaurant's interiors that are groundbreaking. Go for the delicate lace-embroidered curtains; the dim, candle-lit ambience; the French fries served on doilies; the teak-framed, black-and-white photographs; and the achingly charming, antique silver cash register. Go to indulge in what a bistro would look like if designed by Pierre-Auguste Renoir, and enjoy the nostalgic feel with a glass of excellent Beaujolais and a bowl of Provençal beef stew.

6 rue des Tournelles, 75004
Nearest Metro: Bastille
bistrotdestournelles.com

Restaurant
BISTROT DES TOURNELLES

3

LES ARLOTS

Old-school bistronomy and new-wave wines

Natural wine enthusiasts have been flocking to this cosy, bottle-lined bistro ever since rapper-turned-gastronomist Action Bronson showcased its glories on YouTube. Any order must include the trademark saucisse-purée: herbaceous Toulouse-style sausage and velvety mash, drenched in a glossy, umber jus. The menu is classic, and portions are generous, with plenty of creamy oeuf mayo and marbled slices of terrine. Meanwhile, the blackboard offers a rotation of lighter-touch seasonal dishes, such as seared scallops with pumpkin puree and girolles, or amberjack crudo drizzled with olive oil and flecked with hazelnuts. There's bric-a-brac charm and lesser-known wines to marry the hearty fare. Just don't expect any coddling from the wait staff.

136 rue du Faubourg Poissonnière, 75010
Nearest Metro: Barbès–Rochechouart
instagram.com/lesarlots

4

LE CLARENCE

Cutting-edge fine dining in an opulent setting

Fancy cosplaying as an aristocrat? Step into the dining room at Le Clarence, housed in a 19th-century townhouse owned by none other than Prince Robert of Luxembourg. The space is draped in cardinal-red, furnished with damask wallpaper, chandeliers and a library of books as old as the French Revolution. Yet Christophe Pelé's cuisine is strikingly contemporary. The menu shifts daily, pairing pristine seafood with seasonal fruits, herbs, spices and meat, creating novel dishes like Breton Blue lobster with blueberries and bone marrow. If you're going to splurge €150 on lunch, there's no better way to do it than by immersing yourself in this ephemeral world of avant-garde French gastronomy.

31 avenue Franklin Delano Roosevelt, 75008
Nearest Metro: Franklin D Roosevelt
le-clarence.paris

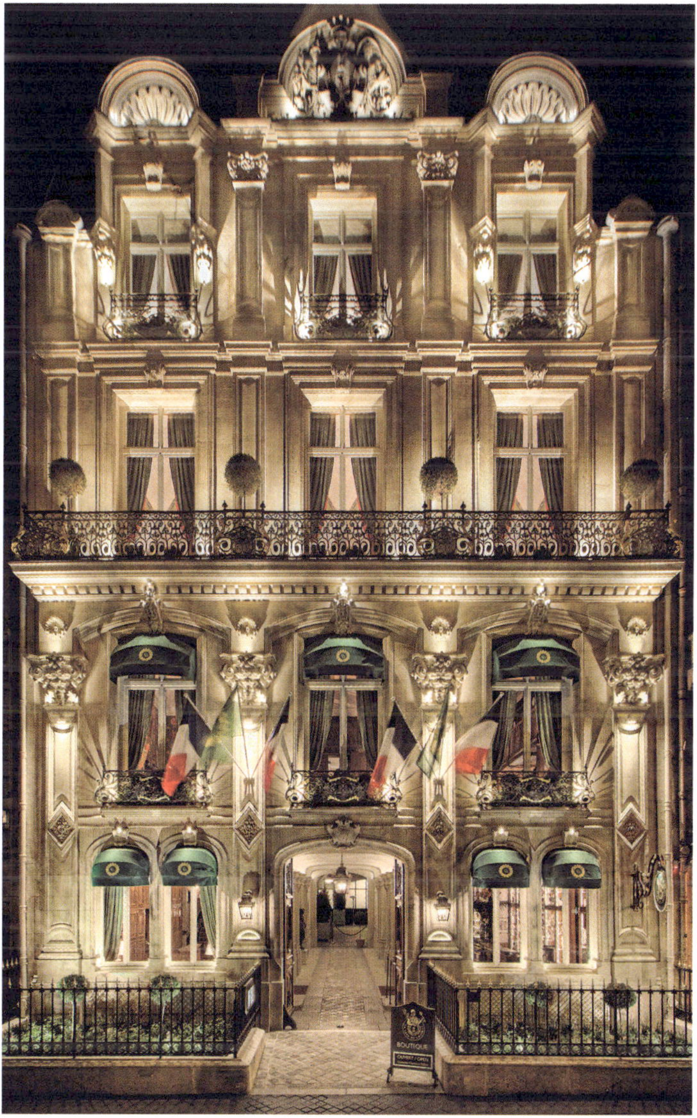

5

CHEVAL D'OR

A Chinese take on the classic French bistro

It's difficult to miss this restaurant's burgundy façade, illuminated by bold, mustard-yellow Chinese characters. The open kitchen is filled with steaming bamboo baskets; a vintage wooden fridge, reminiscent of an older Paris, has been repurposed to store wine. With its down-to-earth, candle-lit class and gutsy but graceful fusion of Cantonese flavours and French technique, Cheval d'Or feels like a genre unto its own, serving up original compositions like prawn-and-crab croque madame or fig clafoutis with red bean and vanilla ice cream as part of two set menu options. The low-intervention wine list is packed with oxidative-edged *vins* that complement the food's complex flavours.

21 rue de la Villette, 75019
Nearest Metro: Jourdain
chevaldorparis.com

6

MAISON SOTA

Weird and wonderful analogue cuisine

Chef Sota Atsumi made his name at the legendary bistro Clown Bar, but at Maison, he has created his own culinary universe. Earthy tones and terracotta tiles give the space its warm, understated elegance, while also acting as an aesthetic realisation of Atsumi's mantra: cooking should be rooted in nature, refined but never overwrought, with no additives or chemical manipulation. A master of classic French sauces, Atsumi employs them in surprising places: a salad of caramelised courgettes, lightly grilled green beans, mizuna (Japanese mustard greens) and pistachio cream might be finished with a sauce albuféra, made with chicken stock, butter and foie gras. A meal at Maison isn't about faux perfection, but memorable moments of strange yet compelling originality.

3 rue Saint-Hubert, 75011

Nearest Metro: Rue Saint-Maur

maison-sota.com

F&M

7

OOBATZ

The best pizza in the city

Inside this low-ceilinged restaurant, American sourdough expert Dan Pearson works magic. Pizzas might be blanketed with a beef ragu that has been cooked for 40 hours, buffalo ricotta or greens, before being blasted for 90 seconds at 400°C, emerging from the oven with beautifully charred crusts, oozing cheese and glistening toppings. Wash it down with a glass of cherry-red pét nat or hazy orange wine from the all-natural list. And while it would be foolish to save room when such brilliant pizza is on offer, your second stomach will be grateful for the indulgent 'pizzookie' – a cookie baked in the pizza oven and topped with vanilla ice cream – that arrives at the table gooey and warm.

4bis avenue Jean Aicard, 75011
Nearest Metro: Rue Saint-Maur
oobatz.fr

8

MAMICHE

Unmissable babka in a bakery worth the queue

The name of this women-run neighbourhood *boulangerie* is displayed in bold, near-fluorescent colours on the window – the first sign that this hip spot stands apart from a classic Parisian bakery. From an excellent jambon and Comté ciabatta sandwich to a stunning range of cookies, buns, croissants and miniature choux pastries studded with rustic sugar icicles, everything is made on-site from top-quality, locally sourced ingredients. The sticky sourdough cinnamon bun and the babka (doughy, marbled and delicately kissed with orange blossom) are unmissable. Queueing is inevitable, but due to popular demand, there are now two more branches in the city.

45 rue Condorcet, 75009

Nearest Metro: Anvers

Other location: 10th

mamiche.fr

BABKA
à la COUPE
le KG

MAMICHE
BOULANGERIE DE QUARTIE
SUMMER
BERRY

9

FOLDEROL

Idiosyncratic natural wine and ice cream bar

Ice cream might not be the first thing you think to pair with a glass of fizz, but it's a surprisingly successful match – the wine's vibrant, fruity bubbles perfectly complement the dairy. Folderol is the kind of meticulously detailed place that distinguishes between sencha (steamed) and hojicha (roasted) tea leaves for its green tea ice cream, and where flavours as varied as spicy watermelon, cornbread, Vietnamese coffee and makgeolli (cloudy Korean rice wine) exist alongside your more conventional pistachio and chocolate. If you're after a glass to accompany your *glace*, you won't find a menu to browse from, but fear not: the knowledgeable staff are on hand to pick and pour something from the cellar, which runs deep with iconic natural wines.

10 rue du Grand Prieuré, 75011
Nearest Metro: Oberkampf
folderol.fr

10

TAPISSERIE

Artisan bakes from one of the city's best restaurants

This bakery from the team behind Michelin-starred Septime (no.13) follows the cult restaurant's philosophy: artisanal but precise. Organic, hand-milled flour provides the base for the pastries, including their signature choux à la flouve: a cream puff with a subtle hay scent achieved by infusing cream with sweet vernal grass. Other baked goods are just as innovative, such as mandarin and saffron tart, or shortcrust pastry with Moroccan amlou and ricotta mousse. Located spitting distance from the restaurant, this pocket-sized site will make you a takeaway coffee to go with your sweet treat.

65 rue de Charonne, 75011

Nearest Metro: Charonne

tapisserie-patisserie.fr

11

CHEZ GEORGES

The quintessential Parisian bistro

Since 1964, this Bourse stalwart has offered a timeless slice of Paris, with chefs clad in classic tall hats, blunt waiters, cosy banquettes and tables draped in white cloth and crammed together like tinned sardines. Proceedings are simple. Attempting to order wine with more specificity than its regional origin might earn you a scowl, but the food makes up for it: escargot arrive with emerald garlic butter bubbling from their shells, entrecôte is gloriously griddled – with unctuous bone marrow scooped onto the meat tableside – while the profiteroles, submerged in molten chocolate sauce, are a fittingly decadent finish. Need any more convincing? Their Instagram is packed with endorsements from their celeb diners, from Anna Wintour to the cast of *Stranger Things*.

1 rue du Mail, 75002
Nearest Metro: Bourse
instagram.com/chezgeorgesruedumail

chez Georges
epuis 1964

12

ROBERT ET LOUISE

Timeless French comfort food

The phrase 'If it ain't broke, don't fix it' rings true at this family-run restaurant turning out plates of hearty Gallic home cooking. Start with the menacing-looking boudin noir (blood sausage): despite appearances, it's lusciously creamy inside and served with a vivacious apple sauce. Next comes the chunky côte de boeuf (bone-in ribeye steak), which you can watch sizzle on a wood-fired grill installed in 1962. The nearly-blue beef arrives at the table with home-style roast potatoes and Dracula-repellent garlic green beans. The space is just as rustic as the food, from the charming granito-tiled floors to side panels painted with flowers. For the full experience of the primal spectacle on offer, book early and secure a seat upstairs in front of the fire.

64 rue Vieille du Temple, 75003
Nearest Metro: Rambeteau
robertetlouise.com

RESTAURANT
Robert et Louise

13

SEPTIME

Revolutionary cuisine and rare wines

Faded organic wood, staff in workwear-style blue jackets and *vins naturels* in every shade set the scene at this Michelin-starred spot in the heart of the 11th. The atmosphere is laid-back, but the food is nothing short of awe-inspiring. Septime has led the sea change in French cuisine over recent decades, offering a monthly-changing tasting menu driven by hyper-seasonal produce and global influences. The optional wine pairing features bottles so rare you'll likely never see them again; perhaps an almost-neon oxidative orange from Roussillon alongside slowly grilled endive crowned with a slice of gossamer-thin lardo, served with a lustrous chicken and walnut jus. Word to the wise: reservations for the following month open at 10am daily and are snapped up immediately, so be ready on the hour.

80 rue de Charonne, 75011

Nearest Metro: Charonne

septime-charonne.fr

14

MARCHÉ DES ENFANTS ROUGES

Paris's oldest food market reinvented

Established in 1615, this is the city's oldest covered market. Originally focused on fresh produce and artisanal goods, it's since been transformed into a bustling food court, with stalls serving Moroccan couscous, Japanese bento boxes, galette rolls, croque monsieurs and Creole pepper bonbons. Natural wine enthusiasts should head to Les Enfants du Marché, where brilliantly creative small plates of seafood – sea urchin with beetroot cream, or smoked eel paired with foie gras and purple turnips – accompany an impressive selection of low-intervention wines. Come hungry, and leave with lighter pockets, heavier waistlines and a satisfying haze.

39 rue de Bretagne, 75003
Nearest Metro: Filles du Calvaire

BIO COMPLET
400g 2,95€

15
SOCES

Seafood with a side of neighbourhood buzz

Nestled in the hilltop centre of Belleville known as 'Village Jourdain', this unmissable eatery dazzles with serious culinary pedigree and an effortlessly cool vibe. The icy seafood display – a tribute to brasseries of a bygone era – features electric-orange spider crabs, spiky purple sea urchin, stacks of oysters and other fresh treasures from the deep. Chef Marius Péan de Ponfilly has a knack for unusual flavour combinations, like creamy beef tartare topped with peppy pike roe. Wash it all down with some *pur jus* ('pure juice', a.k.a. natural wine) from the all-star list. If you're solo or a couple, the bar is a perfect perch for soaking up the lively atmosphere.

32 rue de la Villette, 75019
Nearest Metro: Jourdain
soces.fr

16

LE SERVAN

Bistronomy at its best

The concept of 'bistronomy' burst onto Paris's dining scene in the '90s, marrying high-end culinary finesse with bistro informality. Le Servan perfects the formula. At the helm of this pretty restaurant is chef Tatiana Levha, a master of both flavour and plate design. Start with the boudin noir (blood sausage) wontons – a menu mainstay since Servan's opening in 2014 and one of the single best bites in the city. What follows always involves impeccable, bright cooking. From a flamingo-pink veal tartare with smoked vinegar mayo and dashi jelly, to lobster ravioli in a canary-yellow saffron butter and chilli peanut sauce, you'll be sure to leave with your eyes dazzled and your stomach satisfied.

32 rue Saint-Maur, 75011
Nearest Metro: Voltaire
leservan.fr

Le Servan
RUE St MAUR

17

DELICATESSEN PLACE

Rising culinary stars and artisan Champagne

The 11th arrondissement certainly isn't short of wine bars, but Delicatessen Place offers more than the classic formula of cheese, charcuterie and olives. Many of the city's rising chefs pass through this kitchen, cooking up exquisite plates of raw fish crudo or fresh pasta. Sundays buzz with industry folk, but it's often busy, so arriving shortly after opening is a wise idea. There's no obligation to eat, though; pick up a bottle from the *cave* next door (corkage starts at a modest €10), or order by the glass. Aside from an all-star cast of sought-after natural wine labels, they boast one of Paris's best selections of artisanal, biodynamic and organic Champagne.

7 rue Jean-Pierre Timbaud, 75011
Nearest Metro: Oberkampf
instagram.com/delicatessenplace

DELI CATESSEN
PLACE
Ça bat libre
Mon Blanc
orangé

18

AT

Cross-cultural culinary exploration

The initials in the name stand for Atsushi Tanaka, the Japanese chef–owner of this celebrated eatery. The space is minimalist – all grey-washed walls and thoughtfully sourced ceramics – and the cuisine is masterful. The menu weaves French, Spanish, Nordic and Japanese influences into vivid compositions built around one or two core ingredients, like a centrepiece of lobster tail, grilled to perfection, its claws turned into a gorgeous salad and its shell into an umami bisque-infused chawanmushi (Japanese savoury custard). The natural wine selection satisfies dedicated funk-seekers while offering approachable options for newcomers.

4bis rue du Cardinal Lemoine, 75005
Nearest Metro: Cardinal Lemoine
atsushitanaka.com

19

LE BISTROT PAUL BERT

Legendary for a reason

Warm gougères (cheese choux pastries) land on tables, jovial waiters pin hand-written tickets at the kitchen window and owner Bertrand Auboyneau often appears to greet guests personally. There are no small plates in sight at this Paris institution, which offers generous portions of offal (brain, marrow, foie gras) alongside classics like filet au poivre elevated with woody Sarawak pepper. One dining area is white-tableclothed and lamplit; the other is a more casual affair, the copper-studded walls lined with posters. Complimentary canelés arrive with the cheque, but that's no reason to skip the impossibly airy Grand Marnier soufflé. Opened in the late '90s, the cellar is full of older vintages. Reservations are by phone only.

18 rue de Paul Bert, 75011
Nearest Metro: Faidherbe–Chaligny
bistrotpaulbert.fr

LE BISTROT
PAUL BERT

20

OTTO

Izakaya meets wine bar

The rue Mouffetard area, dominated by tacky tourist spots, has long been known for its scarcity of quality wine bars and restaurants. Thank god for Otto, which is both: a tapas-style menu designed by a Michelin-starred chef and a gold-paged wine list. Styled like an izakaya – a casual Japanese eatery – with bar stools lining the central open kitchen, you can watch meat and veggies come to life over the kiss of traditional Binchōtan coals. The menu is eclectic, from Asia-inflected dishes like grilled shrimps in satay sauce to Gallic plates of razor clams in garlic butter or a sophisticated ballotine of morel-stuffed quail, finished on the grill and smothered in a creamy sauce.

5 rue Mouffetard, 75005
Nearest Metros: Cardinal Lemoine, Place Monge
instagram.com/ottomouffetard

21

L'ARPAON

Intimate neo-bistro away from the crowds

Travelling to the end of Metro Line 4 for dinner better be worth the trek. The good news is that behind the emerald-green velvet curtains marking the entrance to L'Arpaon awaits cooking that is nothing short of spectacular. Founded by three pals, all with unlikely backgrounds in advertising, this refined neo-bistro has all the touches you might expect from a hip eatery – posh Le Labo hand lotion, dried flowers, ceramic decorations – but it wouldn't matter if it didn't. From the gently charred and expertly cooked langoustines with smoked salt and amba mayonnaise, to the chocolate fondant with an oozing centre and salty coconut topping, the flavours are bold – ambitious, even – and *boy*, do they work.

57 rue Montcalm, 75018
Nearest Metro: Porte de Clignancourt
larpaon.com

22

LA MAISON D'ISABELLE

The best croissant in Paris

This celebrated *boulangerie* – named after its owner, Isabelle Leday – gained fame after winning the prestigious Best Butter Croissant in Paris award in 2018. Is it worth the hype? *Absolument*. The classic croissant has an improbably crunchy shell and an interior so buttery it lingers on the palate like a fine white Burgundy wine. Prefer your pastries pimped with almonds and chocolate? The viennoiserie is top-tier across the board, and anything you pick up is sure to boast a similarly perfect contrast. If it's sunny, head to nearby Square Paul Langevin to enjoy your treat from a bench (and try not to worry about the trail of flakes you've left behind).

47ter boulevard Saint-Germain, 75005
Nearest Metro: Maubert–Mutualité
la-maison-disabelle.foodjoyy.com

23

RUINE

An art-forward coffee shop

Ruine is the kind of coffee shop you can only find in Paris. Small, hyper-independent and imbued with genuine enthusiasm: owner Jordan Biermann spent a year soaking up Sydney's coffee culture, followed by a stint at uber-stylish Café Kitsuné, before opening his own joint. Everything is custom-made, from the tables crafted from repurposed boxes to the benches and artwork. Biermann will even let you hang your own art on his walls (there are pots full of coloured pencils and felt-tips on the tables). With regular in-store drawing sessions and a meme-heavy Instagram account, Ruine are too friendly to be a magnet for serious coffee snobs – but they serve top-quality beans all the same.

2 passages du Jeu de Boules, 75011
Nearest Metro: Oberkampf
instagram.com/ruinecoffee

RUINE
COFFEE

24

CANDLE KIDS COFFEE

Quirky neighbourhood cafe

Located inside a cream-coloured corner building that feels uniquely Parisian, this minimalist cafe is calm, airy and bright – a perfect pit stop in which to open a dog-eared copy of Baudelaire and think about a Paris that once was. The design is elegant – washed concrete walls, minimalist paper lampshades and plenty of glossy wood – and there's an eclectic range of homemade sweet treats to go with your flat white. Whether you're after a matcha cookie, Swedish cinnamon bun or a caramelised canelé (only available at weekends), it's all picture-perfect – and immensely tasty.

107 rue des Couronnes, 75020
Nearest Metros: Pyrénées, Jourdain
instagram.com/candlekidscoffee

25

TANAT

Trailblazing coffee roasters

Renowned among speciality coffee aficionados across the globe, Tanat (formerly Kawa) is spearheading the 'fourth wave' of coffee culture in Paris. Wondering what the fourth wave is? Much like what post-punk is to punk, this admittedly hard-to-define label is flung at all sorts of zeitgeisty cafes. At Tanat, it means innovation guides everything – most notably their coffee beans, which are co-fermented with fruit to create a complex, juicy, completely inimitable brew. You can enjoy their vast offering at a few spots in the city, but none is more pleasing than the avenue Victoria location (voted Europe's Best Independent Coffee Shop in 2024), complete with a steel bar, crisp, Virgil Abloh-designed speakers and the signature display of nifty coffee-making paraphernalia.

22 avenue Victoria, 75001
Nearest Metro: Châtelet
Other locations: 2nd, 3rd
tanat.coffee

CORTADO
FLAT WHITE
LATTE

26

POGET & DE WITTE

Oyster heaven

Lyrical food writer M.F.K. Fisher lived in Dijon in the early 1930s, drawn to France for its culinary pedigree. Afterwards, she wrote *Consider the Oyster*, a tribute to the salty treasures she described as 'a thing of earth, sea, and air and of perfect, simple beauty'. At Poget & De Witte, her words ring true. This compact bar is the place to slurp down a variety of oysters: some briny and intense, others as silky – and almost as sweet – as a crème caramel. If you're after a broader seafood feast, order the platter including whelks, sea urchins and cured fish. Legendary bottle shop L'Etiquette is just across the street, and well worth a visit.

5 rue Jean du Bellay, 75004
Nearest Metro: Point Marie
poget-dewitte.com

27

NONETTE BÁNH MÌ & DONUTS

A killer combo

There's been plenty of hype around Nonette's playful twists on the Vietnamese bánh mí – from the VFC (Vietnamese Fried Chicken) to Cheffe's Special, which adds a thick layer of butter to the pork cold cuts, pâté, fresh herbs and pickles, creating a sort of bánh mí/jambon-beurre hybrid. The main draw, though, is the doughnuts. The most ambitious of these spongy, fried balls is topped with pork floss, Chantilly cream and chilli oil, but the *pièce de résistance* is the Kaya doughnut, filled with a silky, salty-edged cream made from coconut and pandan. Can't get enough? Nonette's mother business, The Hood, is just across the street, serving the Kaya cream on everything from toast to croissants.

71 rue Jean-Pierre Timbaud, 75011
Nearest Metro: Parmentier
nonettebanhmi.com

28

CARACTÈRE DE COCHON

Customisable jambon-beurre

No great sandwich exists without great bread. One glance at the profoundly artisanal baguettes at this sandwich spot is all it takes to know the blueprint is there. Charismatic Madagascan owner Solofo 'Solo' Raveloson enjoys chatting to his customers, which is why he only allows one group in at a time. He'll crack a couple of jokes, invite you to choose from a gorgeous range of ham, perhaps add Comté or another cheese and then send you on your way with a mouthwatering jambon-beurre stuffed like a New York deli sandwich. Elie Wiesel Square is conveniently nearby, with plenty of benches that are perfect for chomping it down.

42 rue Charlot, 75003 Paris
Nearest Metro: Filles du Calvaire
instagram.com/caracteredecochonparis

29

ROND

Galettes and apple-based alcohol

Few meals are more comforting than a galette: a crisp buckwheat pancake filled with homely French ingredients. Rond serves some of the best in the city. Opt for the charmingly titled Bizou (meaning 'kiss'), simply filled with goat's cheese and honey, or a hearty *complète* of ham, Comté and fried egg. Elsewhere on the menu, you'll find Roquefort, confit onions or smoked salmon. Thirsty? There's a brilliant selection of artisanal ciders and calvados. *Still* hungry? For dessert, there are perfectly crafted crêpes – lemon and butter for the purists, or decadent salted caramel. Inside is cosy and low-lit, with a sizable terrace for sunnier days.

21 rue du Transvaal, 75020

Nearest Metros: Pyrénées, Jourdain

LA REINETTE
CIDRE DU PERCHE
BRUT
- AOP CIDRE DU PERCHE -
PRÉAUX-DU-PERCHE

30

LE BARATIN

An offaly good bistro

Rumours of head honcho Raquel Carena's impending retirement instil fear in the hearts of Parisian gourmands, for the 'queen of offal' – as she is known colloquially – can cook a cervelle de veau (calf's brain) like no one else. Sometimes her innards cookery gets innovative (cod tripe ragù or kidneys in coffee sauce, anyone?), but mostly it's about respecting the simple purity of French country cooking. Head here while you can to taste Carena's phenomenal menu alongside a bottle from the excellent Loire-heavy natural wine list – and hope that Le Baratin's charm, with its burgundy-red banquettes, old wine maps and model ships, may live on.

3 rue Jouye-Rouve, 75020
Nearest Metro: Pyrénées
instagram.com/lebaratinparis

BLANCS
2018 SAUMUR
PUZELAT
RIEFFEL
MONTANET
PETIT
T. CARBO
TISSOT
PETILLANT NATUREL
CHAMPAGNE LASSAIGNE
ROSE
ROUGES
LOIRE P. LAIR
THOUREIL-SAUMUR POUPONNEAU
ARBOIS A & M. TISSOT
BOURGOGNE J.Y. DEVEVEY
ARDECHE H. SOUHAUT
LANGUEDOC
GAILLAC
ROUSSILLON
PENEDES T. CARBO

31

ARTAZART

Curated prints and wall art

Paris doesn't have a shortage of design-savvy shops selling glossy art books and magazines, but none with such a rich collection of prints as Artazart. If your walls at home are looking a little dreary, you're sure to find something you like from one of the many illustrators and photographers stocked here. From striking street photography to sketchy landscapes, colourful city maps to whimsical watercolours, the range is varied and includes work by established as well as up-and-coming artists (the work of Gil Rigoulet, the first official photographer for newspaper *Le Monde*, is a particular boon). Best of all, everything is extraordinarily affordably priced, with signed limited-edition prints starting at around €30.

83 quai de Valmy, 75010
Nearest Metro: Jacques Bonsergent
artazart.com

JOHN
HAMON
LIBRAIRIE
ARTAZART
GALERIE
LA PISCINE

32

MARIN MONTAGUT

Extraordinarily elaborate gifts

Marin Montagut grew up in Toulouse with antique dealer parents, and it shows. From the moment you step inside his boutique – greeted by a cheerful bell, vintage French music and marble-patterned lamps – you're transported into a whimsical world of miniature Parisian landmark ornaments, elaborate tarot decks and pill boxes enticingly shaped like pieces of fruit. The illustrator's delicate, hand-painted designs – inspired by antique souvenirs – adorn mouth-blown glassware, porcelain plates, mugs, notepads and even silk scarves. His signature pieces include framed paper cut-outs and secret storage units disguised as books.

48 rue Madame, 75006

Nearest Metros: Saint-Placide, Rennes

marinmontagut.com

33

À LA MÈRE DE FAMILLE

Time travel via chocolate

Progression meets tradition in the city's oldest chocolate shop, open since 1761 and predating the Republic itself. The current owners emphasise a bean-to-bar philosophy, so you can be sure their cocoa beans have been sustainably and ethically farmed. From the 'Palet Or' – a bar of bitter chocolate ganache sprinkled with gold leaf, following an 1898 recipe – to liqueur chocolates filled with mezcal as well as whiskey, or packets of black sesame-encrusted toucans (praline fingers), everything on these shelves is made with care, precision and a commitment to tradition as well as creativity. Wrapped in the shop's signature tiger-orange ribbon, they make perfect gifts – but you'll probably rather keep them for yourself.

35, rue du Faubourg Montmartre
Nearest Metro: Grands Boulevards
Other locations: several, see website
lameredefamille.com

GRAND ASSORTIMENT
PRUNES FRANÇAISES NOUVELLES
FRUITS CONFITS ET FRUITS SECS POUR COMPOTES
MALAGA
PISTOLES
FIGUES
DATTES

Biscuits
LEFEVRE-UTILE
À LA MÈRE DE FAMILLE
DEPUIS
1761
SPÉCIALITÉ de MIEL & CONFITURES
CONFISERIE
ET
DESSERTS
À LA MÈRE DE FAMILLE
MAISON FONDÉE EN 1761
FABRIQUE
DE
CONFITURES

MAISON FONDÉE EN
CONFISERIE
CHOCOLATERIE
biscuits
LEFEVRE-UTILE
35
VINS FINS DESSERT
9ème ARR
RUE DU FAUBOURG MONTMARTRE
FRUITS SECS
FRUITS CONFITS
CHOCOLATS
THÉS
MAGASIN SPÉCIAL de DESSERTS d'HIVER
FRUITS SECS POUR COMPOTES & RÉGIMES
SPÉCIALITÉ DE MIEL
FABRIQUE DE CHOCOLATS
A LA MERE DE FAMILLE
Mon FONDÉE EN 1761
CONFISERIE ET DESSERTS

34

MERCI

Not your average concept store

Does the world need any more concept stores? Probably not. But then again, most don't fund education in Madagascar, park cherry-red Fiat 500s in their courtyard just begging to be posed with or curate collections so thoughtfully, it'll be nigh on impossible to leave empty-handed. Stocking some of the most-celebrated European labels, the clothes section leans Scandi, but Gallic vibes shine through the chic design of own-brand products like bags and hats (some with the playful slogan, 'non merci'). Need inspiration for your new kitchen or bathroom? Upstairs, you'll find homeware and furniture so on-trend, you'll be booking space on a shipping container to transport it all home.

111 boulevard Beaumarchais, 75003

Nearest Metro: Saint-Sébastien–Froissart

merci-merci.com

MERCI

35

E.DEHILLERIN

A cook's wonderland

Ever dreamed of owning a duck press or a trout kettle? For wannabe Auguste Escoffiers, this iconic kitchen supply shop has nearly every tool you can imagine – and plenty you didn't know existed. A staple on rue Coquillière since 1820, it's more than a museum of gleaming specialist instruments; there's affordable gear to help you recreate escargot, Pommes Anna, fondue and show-stopping bakes, from tarte tatin to madeleines. Your next dinner party guests are in for a surprise.

18–20 rue Coquillière, 75001
Nearest Metro: Étienne Marcel
edehillerin.fr

36

SHAKESPEARE AND COMPANY

Iconic English-language bookshop

There are bookshops and then there's Shakespeare and Company. Steeped in literary history, the original shop was opened by Sylvia Beach in 1919, becoming a hub for the so-called Lost Generation (Hemingway, Fitzgerald, Stein et al.). It was Beach who published James Joyce's *Ulysses* when no one else would, and decades later, in 1951, George Whitman revived the name she had established for his bookshop. Over 30,000 writers and artists – described by George as 'Tumbleweeds' – have rested their heads here, exchanging work for a place to stay and entry into a vibrant literary community. Today, Whitman's daughter (also called Sylvia) runs the fiercely independent shop, which continues to host literary events and concerts.

37 rue de la Bûcherie, 75005
Nearest Metro: Saint-Michel Notre-Dame
shakespeareandcompany.com

THE PAST, PRESENT
AND FUTURE
MINGLE
AND PULL US
BACKWARD, FORWARD,
OR FIX US
IN THE PRESENT.
WE ARE MADE UP OF
LAYERS
CELLS,
CONSTELLATIONS.
ANAIS NIN
Shakespeare and Company Editions
LIVE FOR HUMANITY

37

OFFICINE UNIVERSELLE BULY

A timeless apothecary of beauty and wellness

This global cosmetics brand has shops across Europe and Asia, but none are more enchanting than its Paris flagship, where walnut cabinets showcasing bottles and vials even extend across the ceiling. Beginning as a perfumier over 200 years ago, they now stock over 900 beauty products, from Berber carmine lipstick to handwoven horse-hair brushes. In need of a gift for a loved one? You can have their initials engraved on a tortoiseshell comb or calligraphed onto a bottle of one of Buly's iconic, water-based fragrances. This is their only shop in Paris with an attached cafe – the ideal excuse to linger even longer and savour the wondrous atmosphere.

45 rue de Saintonge, 75003

Nearest Metro: Filles du Calvaire

Other locations: 4th, 6th, 7th

buly1803.com

38

THE ABBEY BOOKSHOP

Warren of second-hand books

This narrow side street – historically a residence for the city's parchment makers – is a fitting locale for one of Paris's best English-language bookshops (its Canadian ownership can't be missed, thanks to the large flag hanging above the doorway). Warmly lit interiors beckon you into a maze of second-hand treasures, books of all genres packed onto shelves and piled high in wobbly stacks (it's a small space, so leave the clunky suitcase at home). From travel guides to paperback fiction, poetry to religion, patient browsers will be rewarded with affordably priced gems and a chat with affable owner Brian Spence.

29 rue de la Parcheminerie, 75005
Nearest Metro: Cluny–La Sorbonne
abbeybookshop.fr

HE ABBEY BOOKSHOP
PARIS
LUNCHEON
MICHAEL
FIONA

39

LEMON STORY

When Montmartre gives you lemons

Despite all the tourists, Montmartre remains one of the city's most charming neighbourhoods. Its winding streets are home to a bounty of indie boutiques keeping the area's once-bohemian spirit alive. Lemon Story – an ode to all things citrus – is one such store. Here, owner Marion Laperche sells the goods from her family's Provençal plantation, turning yuzus, oranges, limes, Meyer lemons, bergamots and Buddha's Hands (citrus fruits so called for their distinctive finger-like shape) into a range of marmalade-style jams, pickles, salts and liqueurs that put limoncello to shame. The latest addition to the stock draws on her Italian heritage: canestrelli biscuits and amaretti infused with vivid Tahiti and Kaffir limes.

1 rue Garreau, 75018

Nearest Metro: Abbesses

lemon-story.com

1
LEMON STORY
PLANTATION
&
FABRICATION
DANS LE SUD
DE LA FRANCE
ARTISANS
MILITANTS
de la QUALITÉ
ALEX MARSEILLE
ALEXANDRE GUES

40

LA CAVE PIGALLE

The finest natural wine

Walk into any independent wine shop in Paris and there's a good chance you'll come out with a bottle of astonishing value, or with a story to tell – but you may have to cut through the fat to find it. At La Cave Pigalle, *every* bottle is carefully considered. The focused selection comprises low-intervention wines from only the most talented winemakers, like electrifying Jura Savagnins or ethereal pinot noirs from new wave Burgundy producers. Browse the oak-wood shelves for both renowned and under-the-radar bottles, and don't hesitate to ask the uncharacteristically chatty staff for guidance. If a bottle sounds so appealing you simply can't wait to crack it open, drink it at the attached next-door bar, 228 Litres, for a small corkage fee.

3 rue Victor Massé, 75009
Nearest Metro: Pigalle
lacavepigalle.fr

41

YVON LAMBERT

Thoughtful bookshop and gallery space

Doubling as a design-led bookshop and exhibition space, Yvon Lambert offers a welcome respite during busy days of *flânerie*. Established in 1967 by the eponymous art dealer, this is the modern aesthete's dream. The space is chock-full of art monographs, fiction, theory and cult zines, from stylish interiors mag *Apartamento* to fashion-focused *Popeye*. For serious collectors, Lambert's 'Bibliophile' selection is a personal curation of rare artist books, available for viewing by appointment. Behind the bookshop is a small gallery hosting mixed-media shows from a roster of emerging artists and publishers. Pick up a David Shrigley mug or a trademark Lambert tote bag from the gift section on your way out.

14 rue des Filles du Calvaire, 75003

Nearest Metro: Filles du Calvaire

yvon-lambert.com

DETOUR, THE
TROUTH
EVERY PERSON IN NEW YORK
WINE IN

42

PAPIER TIGRE

Brilliantly bold stationery

Upper Marais offers a refreshing escape from the chaos of its falafel-packed, museum-crawling counterpart. Home to shops that champion craftsmanship, Papier Tigre is the standout, founded by graphic designer Maxime Brenon. You'll find everything from handcrafted stationery and bold planners to colourful pens and customisable notebooks (choose between blank, ruled, graph or dot grid paper and select your vibrant cover and binding – all handmade in-house). For the dedicated enthusiast, ready-made notebooks for watercolours, travel journals, projects or reading notes await. And if the city's culinary scene sparks your imagination, grab a pad to jot down recipes, complete with a calendar of seasonal produce.

5 rue des Filles du Calvaire, 75003
Nearest Metro: Filles du Calvaire
papiertigre.fr

La grille
week

43

BONJOUR JACOB

Zine mecca with great coffee

The pinnacle of neo-hipster Paris, offering the holy trinity of single-origin coffee, alternative magazines and punchy art exhibitions, Bonjour Jacob is a slick concept store in the creative northern stretch of Canal Saint-Martin. Uber cool and carefully curated it may be, but this is also the best place to browse inspiring indie publications – whether underground fashion mag *Nylon*, food writing at *Table* and *Serviette* or anthologies of experimental fiction. Keep an eye on their Instagram for event details, which cover everything from magazine launch parties to in-store yoga classes.

28 rue Yves Toudic, 75010
Nearest Metro: Jacques Bonsergent
Other locations: 6th, 9th
bonjourjacob.com

Whatevr
Interview
EXHIBITION
LAM
POON
FARE
FARE
FARE
MONOCLE
CANAL
STREET
ROASTERS

44

SMALLABLE

Sustainable style for all ages

Welcome to the boutique where kids walk out looking cooler than their parents. We're talking little ones donning pint-sized Chelsea boots and cottagecore-style gingham dresses. This concept store champions brands devoted to quality craftsmanship and ethical practices, and while the focus is on creative, sustainable garb for children (like Bobo Choses and Mini Rodini), there are plenty of options for adults, too. It isn't all clothes, either; they also sell homeware, from kids' bed linen to desks, mirrors and home fragrances. Naturally, there's a comprehensive range of children's toys – all from eco-friendly brands – including luxury dolls' houses, imaginative outdoor games and tool sets that encourage learning through play.

81 rue du Cherche-Midi, 75006

Nearest Metro: Vaneau

smallable.com

45

LA SOUFFLERIE

Mouth-blown recycled glassware

Always dreamed of sipping from a glass shaped like a human head? Perhaps not, but holding one in your hands will soon change your mind. The Angelo technique, employed by husband-and-wife team Sébastien and Valentina Nobile, uses plaster moulds based on 200-year-old monk head sculptures from the church of Saint-Sulpice to create unique drinking vessels from 100 per cent recycled materials. This is just one example of the characterful glassware found in this enchanting shop; the Nobiles also sell vases, bowls, cake stands, carafes, cutlery, incense holders and more, all mouth-blown without the assistance of machinery. The couple have also founded a separate non-profit company, with proceeds supporting glassblowers in the hope of keeping this ancient craft alive.

7 rue de l'Odéon, 75006
Nearest Metro: Odéon
lasoufflerie.com

46

LA TRÉSORERIE

Bountiful homeware

This bright, airy store is packed with high-quality homeware labels, all chosen with a focus on craft and provenance. Stock includes 100 per cent linen tea towels from Lapuan Kankurit, vintage-style kouglof moulds and Trésorerie's own line of crockery, which is made in Portugal and comes in a selection of soft, muted colours worthy of a Farrow & Ball paint chart. Much of the selection is French, with iconic kitchen brands like Opinel and Charvet, but they also stock Japanese ceramics, Italian pasta makers and Spanish chopping boards. Don't miss the bathroom section tucked in a corner, which has a scent so relaxing, you'll think you've wandered into a spa.

11 rue du Château d'Eau, 75010
Nearest Metros: Jacques Bonsergent, République
latresorerie.fr

47
BARTHÉLEMY

The city's best fromage

This shop is a contender for the most beautiful facade in Paris, and unquestionably home to its most beautiful cheese display. Beyond the cream-coloured entrance are hundreds of equally creamy cheeses, lined up artfully on porcelain platters and marble shelves. From ash-dusted goat's cheeses that resemble ancient stone tablets, to impossibly tempting golden-rinded raw cow's milk varieties, this is French *fromage* at its most dangerously smooth and complex. For a guaranteed hit at your next cheese and wine evening, opt for the tangy, velvety Rouelle du Tarn, the radiantly luxuriant Gorgonzola and the gloriously crystallised aged Comté, which are sure to elicit gasps of pleasure in your guests.

51 rue de Grenelle, 75007
Nearest Metro: Rue du Bac

CRACKERS AU FROMAGE 6,15€
CONFIT DE CIDRE 5,95€
Fourme de Montbrison
30,40 €
Fourme d'Ambert

48

DEALEUSE

Luminous design

A spectacular diversity of materials, forms and inspirations make up the lighting collection at this chic homeware shop, which sells everything from luxurious, gilded château-style chandeliers to contemporary suspended marble lights and organic-looking floor lamps. Owner Alix is an interior designer passionate about vintage furniture and crafts, and many of her custom lampshades feature lighting fixtures made from repurposed objects. There's an equally thoughtful selection of ornate mirrors, tables, glassware, candles and more. If the shop gives you home envy, seek out Alix's bespoke decor and lampshade services for some expert intel.

7 rue de Vintimille, 75009
Nearest Metro: Place de Clichy
dealeuse.com

49

CENTRE COMMERCIAL

Antidote to fast fashion

Supporting independent, heritage brands before it was cool, Centre Commercial stocks a bumper range of stylish, ethically driven clothing. Whether you're after colourful knitwear by French label Surprise, leather jackets from Cawley or Japanese bags from Porter-Yoshida & Co., you can be certain that everything on these rails has been made with the planet in mind. Perfume, ceramics and even a minimalist tin of olive oil (a collaboration with Olea Pia) make covetable gifts, while the dedicated kids' store is a two-minute walk around the corner on rue Yves Toudic.

2 rue de Marseille, 75010

Nearest Metro: Jacques Bonsergent

Other locations: both in 10th

centrecommercial.cc

50
MUSÉE D'ORSAY

Impressive temple to Impressionism

A trip to Paris would be incomplete without standing in front of Van Gogh's last self-portrait, soaking up its chalky blues and swirling textures. The Musée d'Orsay has two rooms of the artist's work, plus a bevy of other Impressionist and post-Impressionist heavyweights (Cézanne, Monet, Bonnard and more). Temporary exhibitions highlight the museum's strengths in modern and contemporary art, with recent shows including the first-ever retrospective of Christian Krohg's empathetic portraits outside Scandinavia, or the dreamy landscapes of Lucas Arruda. But really, it's worth visiting for the building alone: a Belle Époque-era train station with a striking parabolic roof that floods the expansive interior with light.

Esplanade Valéry Giscard d'Estaing, 75007
Nearest Metro: Solférino
musee-orsay.fr/en

PARIS-ORLEANS

51

LE LOUVRE

Beyond the Mona Lisa

Let's face it, the city's most famous museum can be overwhelming. You might have more fun on the Metro during rush hour than battling your way through crowds to see the *Mona Lisa*, which is why a little strategy goes a long way. The museum runs three different tours in English; the daily highlights tour offers a solid overview, but if you're looking for something different, try *Another Louvre*, held on Mondays, Fridays and Saturdays. It steers you off the beaten path to quieter corners, like the phenomenal (and overlooked) sculpture section. With the kids? Try *Louvre Family*, a child-friendly exploration focused on adventure and storytelling, with visual aids to keep young minds engaged. It's offered on Thursdays, Saturdays and Sundays.

Rue de Rivoli, 75001
Nearest Metro: Palais Royal–Musée du Louvre
louvre.fr

52

BOURSE DE COMMERCE

Stunning contemporary art hub

Home to one of the most enviable private art collections in the world – belonging to business-man François Pinault – this captivating space is a must-visit for contemporary art fanatics. Originally a commodities exchange (hence the name), the grand 18th-century building was redesigned by renowned Japanese architect Tadao Ando, who introduced striking modernist features (the juxtaposition between the concrete inner circle of the main hall and the Beaux-Arts fresco above it is spectacular). The Bourse de Commerce has a reputation for cutting-edge curation and brave, multimedia shows spotlighting major artists from the collection, from Louise Bourgeois to Georg Baselitz and Antonio Obá.

2 rue de Viarmes, 75001
Nearest Metro: Les Halles
boursecommerce.art

53

MUSÉE PICASSO

Journey into the mind of a genius

Many assume Barcelona is the ultimate destination for all things Picasso, but this museum holds the world's largest public collection of the revolutionary artist's work – fitting, given that he spent most of his life in France. The collection is mighty: hundreds of paintings and sculptures – spanning everything from his early sketches to seminal works like *Le Baiser (The Kiss)* – plus thousands of letters, photographs and other archival treasures. Grappling with Picasso's legacy as much as his own work, the dynamic exhibition programme also spotlights artists inspired by the man himself, with recent shows on Jackson Pollock and Sophie Calle.

5 rue de Thorigny, 75003
Nearest Metro: Saint-Paul
museepicassoparis.fr

54

MUSÉE DE L'ORANGERIE

Compact museum of modernist masters

It's most famous as the home of Monet's hypnotic water lily murals – eight panels stretching across the walls of twin oval rooms – but the Musée de l'Orangerie is so much more than this. The permanent collection downstairs delivers a punch of modernist heavyweights: Matisse at his most seductive, Cézanne at his most picturesque and Soutine (the master of painting flesh, known for his series of gutsy beef carcasses) at his most brilliantly gruesome. Like most of Paris's national museums, it's free on the first Sunday of each month.

Jardin des Tuileries, 75001
Nearest Metro: Concorde
musee-orangerie.fr

Orangerie

55

NOTRE-DAME

Revived from the flames

We all remember the haunting images of the city's most iconic cathedral engulfed in flames in 2019. The inspiration for Victor Hugo's *The Hunchback of Notre-Dame*, the building's Gothic flying buttresses and luminous stained glass have been carefully transformed from ruin to their former glory. The painstaking restoration of the building has blended medieval techniques with cutting-edge safety upgrades, requiring the labour of hundreds of artisans to cut and fit 1,000 cubic meters of limestone, shape 2,000 French oak trees into beams using traditional axes and remake the iconic spire – lost in the fire – from 4,000 square meters of lead. Now reborn with purpose and renewed energy, it's not to be missed.

6 Parvis Notre-Dame – Place Jean-Paul II, 75004
Nearest Metro: Saint-Michel–Notre-Dame
notredamedeparis.fr/en

56

POMPIDOU CENTRE

Futuristic cultural hub

Clad in brightly painted pipes and steel scaffolding, the Pompidou is a building turned inside-out (literally – the heating and air-conditioning ducts are on the exterior). The futuristic design was daring for Paris, notorious for its strict building rules – and the centre remains just as radical today thanks to a multidisciplinary programme of exhibitions, debates, workshops and concerts. The permanent collection of modern art is a must-visit, the bookshop is exceedingly well stocked and you shouldn't leave without taking the elevator snaking across the building's facade to the panoramic viewing platform. (The Pompidou will be closed for five years from September 2025 for a renovation, but it's too important to leave out – and worth visiting the square to gawp at the groundbreaking building.)

Place Georges-Pompidou, 75004
Nearest Metro: Rambuteau
centrepompidou.fr

57

PALAIS DE TOKYO

Radical art museum

Viewed from the main road outside, the museum is an awe-inspiring vision of Roman-style grandeur; inside, it's a hyper-contemporary Brutalist space. The building's vast stained-glass windows are periodically redesigned by artists, with previous projects by abstract, Kandinsky-esque Renée Levi and Pop Artist Christian Marclay. The museum's exhibitions champion alternative, cutting-edge art, from Afrofuturism and collective joy to inter-species worlds – with outreach initiatives that engage young people and artists who often work in public view. The expansive, inclusive bookshop – showcasing collections of graffiti, African art and critical theory – reflects the museum's radical spirit: a *palais* for everyone.

13 avenue du Président Wilson, 75116
Nearest Metro: Iéna
palaisdetokyo.com

JUSTICE FOR
BRIAN DOUGLAS
JUSTICE NOW
VICTORIA CLIMBIE FAMILY CAMPAIGN
REMEMBER
VICTORIA CLIMBIE
1991–2000
VICTORIA'S CRIES FOR HELP WERE IGNORED AND THEN THE NIGHTMARE BECAME A REALITY....SHE WAS KILLED
'Always loved, forever smiling but betrayed by the authorities. We can Only promise her justice.'
Tel. 07903 614 265
Tel. 0208 571 4121
JUSTICE CAMPAIGN

58

PASSAGE DES PANORAMAS

Antiquated covered passageway

Paris's oldest arcade once housed immersive, panoramic paintings of world-famous cities – scenes that hinted at the future of cinema and inspired the city's writers grappling with the onset of modernity, like Honoré de Balzac and Émile Zola. For a glimpse of the past, wander into the shop Maréchal and browse postcards, stamps and old photographs; gaze at the intricate woodwork above the restaurant Canard & Champagne, and stop by Caffè Stern, an Italian restaurant which still boasts an original amber marble facade (alongside some questionable taxidermy). The historic space now houses celebrated dining spots like Racines and Club Cochon, where the charm of eating in an arcade adds to the culinary experience.

11 boulevard Montmartre, 75002
Nearest Metro: Grands Boulevards

Timbres
de
collection
Phila2000
BISTROT 70
DIRECT
PRODUCTEURS
PLATS MAISON - SALADES
RACINES
MARIGNY
PHILATELIE
MESSMER

59

LA SALLE OVALE, BNF

Magnificent reading room

The French National Library has several locations, but the site at Richelieu is the most rewarding to visit, offering a museum, a cafe by cult-favourite Rose Bakery and an abundance of reading rooms. Many require academic credentials, but the most stunning is freely accessible to all. Desks are laid out beneath a breathtaking oval dome that bathes rows of historic books in natural light. This room also boasts the city's largest collection of comics – from Marvel's Stan Lee to French classics like *Astérix* – plus plenty of books in English, including an especially strong music section. Arrive before 10am to secure a spot.

5 rue Vivienne, 75002
Nearest Metro: Bourse
bnf.fr/fr/la-salle-ovale

LONDRES
PARIS

60

SACRÉ-CŒUR

A cliché worth surrendering to

Perhaps more than any other city, Paris's iconic landmarks attract hordes of tourists willing to line up for a selfie. You'll find yourself inadvertently photobombing long before you step inside the dramatic, white travertine walls of Sacré-Cœur Basilica. Sure, you could stay perched on the steps outside, chomping a croissant and bearing witness to one of the city's most spectacular vistas, but the interior is truly magnificent. The church's nucleus is its startlingly ornate ceiling mosaic with Christ at its centre, his enormous, golden heart protruding from his chest. Paris might make you queue for its greatest hits, but some are worth the wait.

35 rue du Chevalier de la Barre, 75018

Nearest Metros: Abbesses, Anvers

sacre-coeur-montmartre.com

61

LES CATACOMBS

From skulls to sculpture

Why would anyone leave the charming streets of the world's most beautiful city to enter a labyrinth filled to the brim with the skeletal remains of over six million Parisians arranged in intricate, artistic patterns? Whether or not you're a history buff or have a taste for the macabre, it's a staggering sight. Initially a limestone quarry used to build the city, this network of subterranean tunnels was repurposed in the 18th century to store human remains overflowing from the cemeteries above ground. The catacombs are nearly 300 km long in their entirety, but only a short 1.5 km section is open to the public (though guided tours sometimes take you into sections normally off-limits).

1 avenue du Colonel Henri Rol-Tanguy, 75014
Nearest Metro: Denfert–Rochereau
catacombes.paris.fr

62

PHILHARMONIE DE PARIS

State-of-the-art concert hall

Picture an orchestra, and you're probably imagining a grandiose opera hall – not an otherworldly mass of gleaming silver. Located in the sprawling Parc de la Villette, the Philharmonie de Paris – which looks more like an alien spaceship than a home of classical music – is a truly spectacular building. And that's before you consider the acoustics; the main concert hall, a vision of white, honey and amber hues and Bauhausian curves, has been designed to maximise sonic quality and produce a deep, immersive sound. Check out the exhibition programme: the impressive space hosts multimedia shows on everything from disco to Marc Chagall's connection to music.

221 avenue Jean Jaurès, 75019
Nearest Metro: Porte de Pantin
philharmoniedeparis.fr

Vill
cité

63

FONDATION LOUIS VUITTON

Progressive exhibitions in Gehry's glass masterpiece

A major cultural hub located in the heart of Bois de Boulogne (no.71), Fondation Louis Vuitton – which takes its name from the fashion brand that sponsors it – hosts some of the most exciting exhibitions in the city. Previous shows have included deep dives into Matisse's *The Red Studio* – collaborating with MoMA in New York City to detail the genesis and history of this single masterpiece – and retrospectives of David Hockney and Mark Rothko. With concerts, family workshops and art performances, there are many reasons to visit – not least to feast your eyes on the iconic sail-like glass structure designed by innovative architect Frank Gehry.

8 avenue du Mahatma Gandhi, 75116
Nearest Metro: Les Sablons
fondationlouisvuitton.fr

64

MUSÉE D'ART MODERNE

Mighty repository of art

Any visit to this museum must begin with *La Fée Electricité*, Raoul Dufy's monumental 600-square-metre mural from the 1937 Exposition Internationale – an electrifying tribute to the role of electricity in modern life, bursting with energetic hues of cobalt, lime, mustard and violet. Then make your way to the Matisse room, where the artist's sloping, pink-and-black dancers come to life on large canvas and in rare archival footage of the artist at work. The permanent collection – free to visit – excels in Cubism, Dada and the borderlines between Impressionism and Expressionism, with show-stopping works by Léger, Picasso, Chagall, Bonnard and more.

11 avenue du Président Wilson, 75116

Nearest Metro: Iéna

mam.paris.fr

65

SAINTE-CHAPELLE

Gothic grandeur

Once part of the Capetian royal palace and home to the King of France until the 14th century, Sainte-Chapelle is one of the oldest surviving buildings on the Île de la Cité – a natural island on the Seine. Over 1,000 soaring stained-glass windows illuminate the chapel in royal blue and purple, depicting scenes from Genesis to the Passion of Christ. The flamboyant rose window and vaulted, gilded ceiling heighten the spectacle. Peek closer and you'll spot intricate carvings, like a Baroque angel perched in the king's alcove and a detailed, stone rendering of Noah's ark. This marvel of Gothic architecture is extremely popular, so booking is essential.

10 boulevard du Palais, 75001
Nearest Metro: Cité
sainte-chapelle.fr

66

MUSÉE RODIN

Sensational sculptures

You might recognise the museum garden's central feature from *Midnight in Paris* – though *The Thinker* hardly needed a cinematic cameo to cement its status as an icon of introspection. Rodin's former home and studio is now an 18-room museum that traces his stylistic evolution towards abstraction and the raw, expressive power of the body, from wonderfully grotesque renderings of Balzac to faceless dancers with arched spines. Come spring – in May especially – the garden's sculptures are brightened by the vivid pink of Rodin roses, a variety specially cultivated for the space. A combined ticket includes the nearby Musée du Quai Branly, housing a large collection of ethnographic objects and Indigenous art.

77 rue de Varenne, 75007
Nearest Metro: Varenne
musee-rodin.fr

67

PÈRE LACHAISE CEMETERY

Reflect on the city's icons

This is the city's largest cemetery, and the final resting place of Chopin, Édith Piaf, Oscar Wilde, Jim Morrison and thousands of others. Stroll through paths lined with maple, chestnut and willow trees, and admire tombs both ordinary and extraordinary. Morrison's gravestone is rather austere, but always heaped with flowers, and you're bound to hear someone playing 'Riders on the Storm' from a tinny phone speaker in tribute. More striking is Jacob Epstein's art deco sculpture, a custom design for Oscar Wilde's tomb that took ten months to complete. Epstein's work is a tribute to Wilde's 174-line poem *The Sphinx*, an ode to sexual liberation that feels suitably eternal in the City of Light.

Père Lachaise Cemetery, 75020
Nearest Metro: Père Lachaise

FAMILLE
BERLOQUIN

68

PETITE CEINTURE

Abandoned railway turned hidden urban escape

Translating as 'Little Belt', this 32-km railway line once circled 19th-century Paris and is now a wild urban escape. You can't walk the whole thing, but large sections of the track have been renovated and are open to the public, home to playgrounds and community gardens, plus overgrown areas where wildflowers, grasses and other plants thrive between the decaying railway ties. Former train stations, like Poinçon in the 14th and Hasard Ludique in the 18th, have been converted into cultural hubs offering food, drinks, live music and art events. The longest walking route can be found in the 12th arrondissement, from rue de Charenton to avenue de Sainte-Mandé: a 1.6-km stretch including a nature trail and garden.

Various access points

petiteceinture.org

69

PARC DES BUTTES-CHAUMONT

A green retreat with staggering views

It's hard to believe such a serene place exists on the edge of some of Paris's grittier neighbourhoods. Depending on where you enter, a waterfall, a pine tree or an aloe vera bush may make you wonder if you're still in the city at all. But stroll the upper ring of this truly breathtaking park and you'll catch sight of apartment blocks peeking out above the foliage. A small lake in the centre surrounds the moss-covered Temple de la Sybille, a Roman-style viewing platform perched atop a cliff like a fairytale castle.

19 avenue Simon Bolivar, 75019
Nearest Metro: Buttes Chaumont

70

PARC RIVES DE SEINE

A 7-km walkway along the river

'Parc' is a misleading description for what is in fact a 7-km promenade along the Seine, stretching from Pont de Sully to Pont de la Concorde on the Right Bank, and Pont de l'Alma on the Left. On the Concorde side, there are weeping willows and a graffiti-plastered underpass. If you fancy nursing a coffee or spritz by the river, Port de la Rapée is home to a fleet of permanently moored boat bars. The Sully side is greener: wide pathways and sculptures nestled amid abundant plant life. Swing by in the early evening, and you may catch a group of loose-limbed salsa or nostalgic *bal-musette* dancers assembled next to the water. Joggers – this is your route.

Pont de Sully, 75005 to Pont de la Concorde, 75007
or Pont de l'Alma, 75008
Nearest Metros: Sully–Morland, Concorde,
Alma–Marceau

71

BOIS DE BOULOGNE

Where nature meets leisure

This 850-hectare park was once a hunting ground for the royals. No longer the preserve of kings and nobility, the vast, leafy expanse now brims with a much broader set of leisure activities. There are 15 km of cycling routes, extensive walking trails, boat rentals and children's play areas. Use one of the many picnic spots for lunch or – for those wanting to indulge in the spirit of the park's opulent past – try the triple-Michelin-starred restaurant Le Pré Catelan. For culture vultures, Fondation Louis Vuitton (no.63) is located on the grounds, and Musée Marmottan Monet – home to the world's biggest collection of his works – is just outside.

Bois de Boulogne, 75016 Paris
Nearest Metros: Porte D'Auteuil, Les Sablons

72

CANAL SAINT-MARTIN

Ever-changing urban waterway

You can experience this century-old canal network on a Seine tour that winds through the historic Bastille vault, but the best way to explore it is by wandering on foot. Stretching from the Bassin de la Villette in the north to the Port de l'Arsenal near the Bastille (though partly passing through a tunnel), this waterway has become synonymous with the city's vibrant urban culture. The liveliest section is from Villette to Square Frédérick Lemaître. Students lounge by the water with Kronenbourgs in hand, Panglossian *pêcheurs* lower their rods and buskers fill the air with rhythmic Moroccan gnawa music. The streets on either side of the canal are peppered with boho cafes and bars; when you're done ambling, grab a croissant or pistachio swirl from the famed Du Pain et des Idées and watch the world go by.

Bassin de la Villette, 75019
to Square Frédérick-Lemaître, 75010
Nearest Metros: Jaurès, Goncourt

73

PARC MONCEAU

A most eccentric green space

Offering a glimpse into the Enlightenment-era fascination with different cultures and epochs, this romantic green space is scattered with a mini Egyptian pyramid, Chinese pagoda, Renaissance-style arcade and, most picturesque of all, a Corinthian colonnade curving around a pond that teems with diverse birdlife. The park's design was inspired by late 18th-century English gardens, and its winding paths are lined with spectacular trees, from Oriental plane – common in Parisian parks – to less typical Lebanese cedars and Chinese-origin ginkgo biloba. Multiple playgrounds make it an ideal destination for families.

Parc Monceau, 75008
Nearest Metro: Monceau

74

GRANDE MOSQUÉE DE PARIS

Moorish tranquility amidst Parisian buzz

Constructed in 1926 with terracotta pieces from Fez, France's first mosque was designed in an Andalusi and Maghrebi style. This means mosaics, cedar-wood arches with intricate geometric carvings, and a zellige-tiled, seafoam-hued courtyard lined with Mediterranean cypress trees. The elaborately designed tearoom is a serene, relaxing respite from the pulse of the city, serving crepes, brik (a thin, stuffed pastry), a range of lime-green pistachio-based sweets and other North African snacks to be washed down with mint tea. There is also a women-only hammam, a tranquil space offering traditional massage and scrubbing services.

2bis place du Puits de l'Ermite, 75005
Nearest Metro: Place Monge
grandemosqueedeparis.fr

75

JARDIN DU LUXEMBOURG

An urban oasis

Nicknamed 'Luco' by the locals, the Jardin du Luxembourg is a sanctuary of calm away from the studenty buzz of the Latin Quarter surrounding it. The manicured Senate gardens burst into a kaleidoscope of colour every spring when the tulips and daffodils come into bloom. Whether basking in the sun or getting lost in a novel, the best way to enjoy this chromatic display is from a free-to-use fern-green reclining chair, found in the park's central open expanse. Cool off by the tree-shaded Medici Fountain; its grand reflective basin leads to a striking sculptural ensemble of Polyphemus spying on Acis and Galatea, a story from Greek mythology.

Jardin du Luxembourg, 75006
Nearest Metros: Luxembourg, Odéon

76

PROMENADE PLANTÉE

Stroll down an elevated path

This walkway stretches 4.7 km from Bastille through to Bois de Vincennes (Paris's largest green space). You should enter from the staircase on avenue Daumesnil, where you can stroll down tree-lined paths, encountering climbing roses, trellised vines and, in the spring, frothy pink cherry blossoms. Also known as the Coulée Verte René-Dumont, the world's first elevated linear park offers views across the city's pretty rooftops and glimpses of top-floor apartments – a (literal) window into Parisian life. Water features add to the charm, with shallow channels and decorative pools integrated into garden beds near the Viaduc des Arts, and a free sparkling water fountain (yes, really) in Reuilly Garden.

11 avenue Daumesnil, 75012
Nearest Metro: Ledru-Rollin

77

JARDIN DES PLANTES

Botanical glory

Unmissable in spring but delightful all year round, the Jardin des Plantes is undoubtedly Paris's most picturesque public space. The park is home to over 10,000 plant species, from forested paths with century-old trees to an expansive lawn where all kinds of flowers and shirotae cherry trees burst into glorious blossom around April. Why such staggering biodiversity? It's both a public park and botanical research centre, so those curious about the science of the natural world won't want to miss the historic greenhouses cultivating endangered tropical plants, as well as the on-site zoo and natural history galleries.

57 rue Cuvier, 75005
Nearest Metros: Gare d'Austerlitz, Jussieu
jardindesplantesdeparis.fr/en

Grand panda
Hyène rayée

78

PLACE DES VOSGES

A historic square worth lingering in

Paris has many squares, but none quite as storied – or elegant – as Place des Vosges. The city's first royal square, once a hangout for French nobility, was renamed after the revolution to honour Vosges, the first region to pay taxes to the new republic. Today, it's more tranquil than grand. Groups lounge on the lawn by the fountains and readers tuck into novels beneath a canopy of trees, their branches pruned into striking sculptural precision. Arched arcades ring the square, lined with quintessentially Parisian cafes, restaurants and galleries.

Place des Vosges, 75004
Nearest Metro: Bréguet–Sabin

79

HOTEL PULITZER PARIS

Where relaxation and style converge

Sometimes an art hotel can be all art and no comfort, but amenities and taste go hand-in-hand at the Pulitzer. The bedrooms are kitted out with plush pillows and ultra-powerful showers, while the verdant patio – part of the lobby's tapas restaurant – is the perfect stage for the hotel's signature cocktail, a zesty French Paradise. From oddly shaped vases and textured lamps to warmly lit Japanese stencil drawings, it's a joyfully maximalist puzzle. The location? Brilliantly strategic, nestled in the vibrant Opera quarter but sheltered from the selfie-stick hordes. For prime people-watching, City View rooms offer bird's-eye glimpses of the hustle and bustle below.

23 rue du Faubourg Montmartre, 75009

Nearest Metro: Grands Boulevards

hotelpulitzer.com

80

GRAND PIGALLE EXPERIMENTAL

Chic base in the city's hippest area

Dotted with indie boutiques, brasseries, no-frills karaoke bars and the occasional neon-lit adult shop (a reminder of the area's seedy history as Paris's red-light district), Pigalle is fast becoming one of the city's hippest neighbourhoods, and this hotel is the ideal base for exploring it. A fever dream of French eccentricity, where leopard-print carpets and old fireplaces clash with bathrooms tiled entirely in blue, every room feels like a stylish friend's apartment – if that friend were a Parisian with impeccable taste in vintage furnishings. And you'll be within easy reach of the hotel's on-site restaurant, Frenchie Pigalle, serving creative fusion dishes from award-winning chef Alaeddine Zitoun. What's not to love?

29 rue Victor Massé, 75009
Nearest Metro: Pigalle
grandpigalle.com

81

LE GRAND MAZARIN

Opulence in the heart of the Marais

With its candy-coloured decor straight out of a Wes Anderson film set and staff in matching purple outfits, a stay at Le Grand Mazarin sometimes feels more like a theatrical performance than a hotel visit. Created by Swedish interior designer Martin Brudnizki, the hotel is a maximalist riot of salmon-pink wardrobes, bespoke Baroque-style tapestries and whimsical scallop-edged rugs. It would be dizzying in the hands of anyone else, but the rooms here are as comfortable as they are flamboyant. Floating in the pool beneath a dreamlike painted ceiling will have you forgetting that you're minutes from the city's busiest streets.

17 rue de la Verrerie, 75004
Nearest Metro: Saint-Paul
grandmazarin.com

Chopin

82

LA FANTAISIE

Fantasy indeed

This hotel is as confident in its delivery as it is in its choice of name. The rooms – ranging from a cosy two-person 'Comfort' to spacious suites – are sunny and elegant, thoughtfully decked out with contemporary art. Despite its location in bustling Montmartre, the rooftop bar is quiet enough to savour the sunset (and also serves a mean French 75), while the verdant open-air garden is the ideal spot to get stuck into a book. The restaurant turns out delicious plates filled with premium seasonal ingredients and impeccable patisserie (the Fantaisie-Brest is a standout). The biggest draw, though, is the spa – a tranquil warren of baths, saunas and a hammam, where you can sweat and plunge to your heart's content.

24 rue Cadet, 75009
Nearest Metro: Cadet
lafantaisie.com

83

LE JARDIN DE VERRE

Stylish aparthotel

Once the haunt of Hemingway and De Beauvoir, today's Latin Quarter, thrumming with bohemian charm, remains one of the most attractive places to rest your head in the city. Enter Le Jardin de Verre, a chic aparthotel with a selection of stylish studios and suites. Designed for travellers who want to feel at home, spaces include private living areas and kitchens – although you'll only be seconds away from the lush atrium restaurant that gives the hotel its name. There's a comfortable co-working area and an on-site boulangerie. And the best bit? You can stay for up to a year.

7 rue Lacépède, 75005

Nearest Metro: Place Monge

lockeliving.com/en/paris/le-jardin-de-verre-by-locke

84

ODÉON THEATRE

Subtitled French theatre

Odéon is committed to sharing the joys of French theatre with non-native speakers – so much so that they're currently testing augmented reality glasses that display multilingual subtitles. Until that launches, they boast an English-language subtitle programme running on Saturdays, featuring plays like *The Seagull* and *Fear and Misery of the Third Reich*. The spectacle begins before the play, when you enter the absurdly beautiful gold-gilded hall, complete with regal Burgundy-red seats and a magnificent ceiling painting of the 12 signs of the zodiac by François-Louis Dejuinne, a swirling kaleidoscope of divinities, arabesques and medallions.

Place de l'Odéon, 75006
Nearest Metro: Odéon
theatre-odeon.eu

85

FRÉQUENCE

Highballs and hard-hitting funk

Stylish stools. Shelves brimming with vinyl. Analogue speakers pumping smooth disco-funk big-hitters. Fréquence is a legendary listening bar shaking up exquisite cocktails to a soundtrack of Atlantic Starr and Michael Wycoff. The highball selection is especially strong, but if fizzy isn't your thing, try the mezcal-engineered Maniu, aromatised with spices and cedro lemon. It's a tiny space, walk-ins only, with weekday nights better suited to solo listeners or intimate dates; come the weekend, though, and tables are cleared away to make space for dancing.

20 rue Keller, 75011
Nearest Metro: Ledru-Rollin
instagram.com/frequenceparis

86

BAR NOUVEAU

Drink in an Art Nouveau dreamscape

This bar may have been opened by some of the biggest names in mixology, but what they pour into glasses almost takes a backseat compared to the frankly ingenious design. The sharp cocktail list is crafted from meticulously sourced, rare spirits, and every inch of this tiny spot has been considered, from the strictly French vintage soundtrack to the curved white marble bar, mottled turquoise walls, mosaic floor and elegant wooden stalls. Catch sight of yourself sipping out of a 1920s Bimini glass (they own the world's largest private collection of them) in the overhead mirror, and you might wonder if you'll ever look this cool again.

5 rue des Haudriettes, 75003
Nearest Metro: Rambuteau
*instagram.com/bar_nouveau_*

87

LE MARY CELESTE

Seafood, cocktails and late-night wine

With its whitewashed wood and pastel-blue hues, this multi-purpose bar in the Marais feels appropriately aquatic for a spot where cocktails and *fruits de mer* go hand-in-hand. On weekends, crowds spill onto the street, lured by the slick, three-ingredient cocktail list that sees whisky, apple and cherry soda become a refreshing Scotch & Soda, or calvados, Cuban honey and miso transformed into a seductive Orchard. For the peckish, there are oysters, whelks and seafood-focused small plates to accompany the drinks. Wine lovers take note: this is one of the only lists in the city that you can order from in the early hours of the morning.

1 rue Commines, 75003 Paris
Nearest Metro: Saint-Sébastien–Froissart
lemaryceleste.com

88

THE CAMBRIDGE PUBLIC HOUSE

World-class cocktails in an unexpected setting

A pub visit might not be on your Paris agenda, but this one's far from your average fusty boozer. Okay, there may be gilt-framed paintings of bucolic English scenes across the establishment walls and sausage rolls for the hungry tipplers, but this is also the best cocktail bar in the city (officially – it was voted number 19 in the World's 50 Best Bars awards in 2024). There are many options on the wildly creative rotating cocktail list, but finishing with Cigarette After Sex – made with hibiscus tea, mezcal and gin – will give you the same satisfaction as its name suggests.

8 rue de Poitou, 75003
Nearest Metro: Saint-Sébastien–Froissart
thecambridge.paris

89

LIQUIDERIE

Get hazy on hazy beers

It can get a little steamy inside this legendary Belleville corner bar, often jam-packed with bearded beer lovers and beret-clad fashionistas alike. The atmosphere gets headier as the night progresses and, after a few rounds from the 20+ taps (14 beers, six wines and a pét nat), you'll be enveloped in a pleasantly hazy fog. Tipples on offer include everything from white Jura wines to French Saison beers, British IPA and Belgian Gueuze (sour beer) from famed producer Cantillon (the Burgundy of the beer world). You can grab a bottle of intriguing natural wine from the fridge – but with pours available in 12.5cl, 25cl and 50cl, it would be a shame not to sample as much of what's on offer as possible.

7 rue de la Présentation, 75011
Nearest Metro: Belleville
Other location: 11th
liquiderie.com

LIQUIDERIE
Artisan
bottle
shop

90

LE BAL BLOMET

Historic jazz club

This Montparnasse jazz bar was once the beating heart of Paris's interwar art scene, where Django Reinhardt's hypnotic guitar melodies and Josephine Baker's exuberant dancing dazzled the likes of Pablo Picasso, Ernest Hemingway and F. Scott Fitzgerald. Today, audiences relive this history with hawk-eyed attentiveness, fully immersed in the music thanks to the bar closing during seated sessions (grab a craft beer or cocktail and some rillettes to snack on prior to kick off). The programme is eclectic, with everything from cabaret, interwar swing and traditional Jewish klezmer music through to Brazilian pop. If you're a French speaker but a jazz novice, try one of *Les 1001 Nuits du Jazz*, where performances are accompanied by explanations of different subgenres.

33 rue Blomet, 75015
Nearest Metro: Volontaires
balblomet.fr

91

MONTEZUMA CAFÉ

Rustic plates and refined sound

Opened in 2019 by Théo de Penanster and Louis Mesana (formerly of natural wine institution Le Verre Volé), Montezuma is inspired by Japanese listening bars, where the focus is on an interesting vinyl collection and high-fidelity sound. Grab a table here to indulge in jazz, soul, and funk with a crystalline purity you simply can't replicate at home. When records aren't spinning from their own collection, it's because they're hosting guest sets from the likes of Haseeb Iqbal and Tash LC. There are home-style plates of spätzle and rabbit stew to accompany the tunes, and – thanks to Mesana's know-how – plenty of natural wine.

15 rue Notre Dame des Victoires, 75002
Nearest Metro: Bourse
montezumacafe.com

MONTEZUMA
CAFÉ

92

BAMBINO

Japan-inspired listening bar

Where streamlined sound meets stylish design, Bambino is a listening bar–restaurant fusion that hits all the right notes. Nibble on wood-fired small plates from Japanese chef Kenta Tomoda and sip on something from the sharp, well-curated drinks menu. The highballs section features Japanese classics like Umeshu and Yuzushu, or you can opt for a Silk, which blends Umeshu, Lutèce and tonic to produce a drink as smooth as the sound system. Teak-wood speakers blast pristine vibrations of disco, funk and boogie, but this is more of a purists' listening bar than a dance spot, so enjoy the tunes perched on a stool at the counter. Drink enough of those potent highballs and you'll be convinced you've teleported to Tokyo.

25 rue Saint-Sébastien, 75011
Nearest Metro: Saint-Sébastien–Froissart
bambinoparis.com

IMAGE CREDITS

Page 2 © Lucas Baba @lucartchivery; page 4 © Hemis / Alamy; page 6 © Aurore Nguyen; page 7 © Romain Ricard; page 8 © Eliott Goutard; page 9 © Jordan Gonzales; Café du Coin all images © Olivia Antonetti / @olivia_atnt; Bistrot des Tournelles © Ashish Uppala / @supershishy; Les Arlots © Lola Piette; Le Clarence © Clarence Dillon; Cheval d'Or all images © Joann Pai; Maison © Daryl Hirsch; Oobatz © Timothée Chambovet; Mamiche all images © Mamiche; Folderol © Lisa Klein Michel; Tapisserie © Lisa Klein Michel; Chez Georges © Lucy Wiffen; Robert et Louise © Brian Eden; Septime © Maurine Toussaint; Marché des Enfants Rouges © Kate Hockenhull / Alamy; Soces © Marius Péan; Le Servan © Virginie Garnier; Delicatessan Place all images © Delicatessan Place; AT © Maurine Toussaint; Le Bistrot Paul Bert © Helena Moursellas; Otto © Sadik Sans Voltaire; L'Arpaon © Ophelie Lebon; La Maison d'Isabelle © Lauren Judd; Ruine © Sylvaine Sansone; Candle Kids Coffee © Matteo Verzini @matteoverzini; Tanat © Maéva Trm; Poget & de Witte © Les Perles Rares; Nonette Banh Mì & Donuts © Aurore Nguyen; Caractère de Cochon © Mathilde Betinas; Rond © Sungbin Kang; Le Baratin © Joann Pai; Artazart © Marin Stefani; Marin Montagut © Romain Ricard; À la Mère de Famille both images © Alexandre Guirkinger; Merci © Robin Ooode; E.Dehillerin © Adam Eastland / Alamy; Shakespeare and Company photo by Hugo Clair Torregrosa © Shakespeare and Company Paris; Officine Universelle Buly © Officine Universelle Buly; The Abbey Bookshop © Raleightillman | Dreamstime.com; Lemon Story © @jaifaim; La Cave Pigalle © @228Litres; Yvon Lambert © Librairie Yvon Lambert; Papier Tigre © Christophe Caudroy; Bonjour Jacob © Daniel Bernard Neuhaus; Smallable © David Foessel, courtesy JCPCDR Architecture; La Soufflerie © La Soufflerie; La Trésorerie © David AROUS; Barthélemy © Stephanie Youngblood; Dealeuse © Alix Rensmann; Centre Commercial © Centre Commercial; Musée d'Orsay first image © F1online digitale Bildagentur GmbH / Alamy, second image © Julian Elliott Photography; Le Louvre first image © Owen Franken, second image © Matej Pribanic; Bourse de Commerce © Marc Domage; Musée Picasso © Stephane Couturier/Artedia / Bridgeman Images; Musée de l'Orangerie first image © Fausto Marci / Alamy, second image © Martin Bache / Alamy; Notre-Dame © naibank; Centre Pompidou © Willi Nuchterlein; Palais de Tokyo © JOHN KELLERMAN / Alamy; Passage des Panoramas © UlyssePixel / Alamy; La Salle Ovale, BNF © Frlegros | Dreamstime.com; Sacré-Cœur © Tuul and Bruno Morandi / Alamy; Les Catacombes © Guy Bryant; Philharmonie de Paris © Thomas Garcia / Alamy; Fondation Louis Vuitton © Atlantide Phototravel; Musée d'Art Moderne © Universal History Archive; Sainte-Chapelle © Roger Viollet Collection; Musée Rodin first image © Aurelie Mole, second image © agence photographique du musee Rodin - Jerome Manoukian, third image © musee Rodin (Photo Cyrille Weiner); Père Lachaise © Wojciech Rzepka; Petite Ceinture © Rames Quinerie; Parc des Buttes-Chaumont © Horizon Images/Motion / Alamy; Parc Rives de Seine © Hemis / Alamy; Bois de Boulogne © John G. Wilbanks / Alamy; Canal Saint-Martin © eric laudonien / Alamy; Parc Monceau © Aide Paulmichl / Alamy; Grande Mosquée de Paris © Leonie Lambert / Alamy; Jardin du Luxembourg © olrat / Getty; Promenade Plantée © Hemis / Alamy; Jardin des Plantes first image © directphoto.bz / Alamy, second image © Hemis / Alamy, third image © Olga Matveeva; Place des Vosges © JOHN KELLERMAN / Alamy; Hotel Pulitzer Paris © Pulitzer Hotels; Grand Pigalle Experimental © Experimental; Le Grand Mazarin both images © vincent leroux; La Fantaisie first two images © Jérome Galland, third image © sergio grazia; Le Jardin de Verre all images © Francisco Nogueira; Odéon-Théâtre © Benjamin Chelly; Fréquence © Fréquence; Bar Nouveau © Audrey Carpentras; Le Mary Celeste © Guillaume Belvèze; The Cambridge Public House © courtesy of The Cambridge Public House; Liquiderie © Harry Blofeld; Le Bal Blomet © Victor Tonelli / Hans Lucas; Montezuma Café © Celia Spenard-Ko; Bambino © Valerio Geraci.

An Opinionated Guide to Paris
First edition, first printing

Published in 2025 by Hoxton Mini Press, London.

Text by Joel Hart
Editing by Florence Ward
Production design by Dom Grant
Production control by David Brimble
Proofreading by Kate Overy
Editorial support by Richard Enright and Flora MacKenzie

With thanks to Matthew Young for initial series design.

Please note: we recommend checking the websites listed for each entry before you visit for the latest information on price, opening times and pre-booking requirements.

Thank you to all of the individuals and institutions who have provided images and arranged permissions. While every effort has been made to trace the present copyright holders we apologise in advance for any unintentional omission or error, and would be pleased to insert the appropriate acknowledgement in any subsequent edition.

A CIP catalogue record for this book is available from the British Library.

ISBN: 978-1-914314-97-1

Printed and bound by OZGraf, Poland

Manufacturer: Hoxton Mini Press, 104 Northside Studios, 16–29 Andrews Road, London E8 4QF, UK
www.hoxtonminipress.com

Represented by: Authorised Rep Compliance Ltd., Ground Floor, 71 Lower Baggot Street, Dublin D02 P593, Ireland
www.arccompliance.com

Hoxton Mini Press is an environmentally conscious publisher, committed to offsetting our carbon footprint. This book is 100 per cent carbon compensated, with offset purchased from Stand For Trees.

Every time you order from our website, we plant a tree:
www.hoxtonminipress.com

Selected opinionated guides in the series:
For more go to www.hoxtonminipress.com

ABOUT HOXTON MINI PRESS

Hoxton Mini Press is a small indie publisher based in east London. We make beautiful books with a dedication to sustainable production and great photography.

When we started the company, people told us print was dead; we wanted to prove them wrong. Books are no longer just about information, but objects to collect and own.

We promise three things. Firstly, nothing in this guidebook is sponsored; it's our own independent opinion. Secondly, our books are 100 per cent carbon compensated with printing, paper and transport fully offset. And finally, everything is researched, edited and written by humans, not AI.

INDEX